BOB ARTLEY's

Memories Of A Former Kid

BOB ARTLEY's

Memories

Of A Former Kid

Once Upon a Time
on the Family Farm

by
BOBARTLEY

Voyageur Press

To Ginny, to Mom, and to the memory of Dad

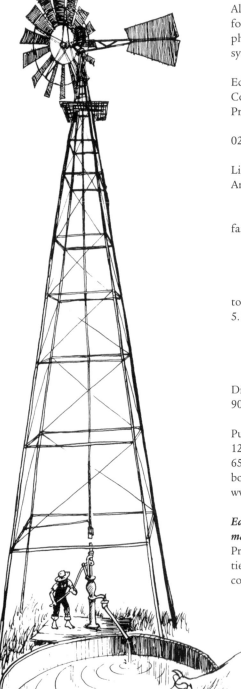

Edited by Floyd Egner
Cover Design by JoDee Turner
Printed in China

02   03   04   05   06   5   4   3   2   1

Library of Congress Cataloging-in-Publication Data
Artley, Bob.
    [Memories of a former kid]
    Bob Artley's Memories of a former kid : once upon a time on the family farm / by Bob Artley.
        p. cm.
    Rev. ed. of: Memories of a former kid. c1978.
    ISBN 0-89658-493-3 (alk. paper)
    1. Artley, Bob—Childhood and youth. 2. Iowa—Social life and customs—20th century. 3. Farm life—Iowa. 4. Country life—Iowa.
5. Iowa—Biography. I. Title.
    F625.42.A78 A78 2002
    977.7'033—dc21
                            2002004757

Distributed in Canada by Raincoast Books
9050 Shaughnessy Street, Vancouver, B.C. V6P 6E5

Published by Voyageur Press, Inc.
123 North Second Street, P.O. Box 338, Stillwater, MN 55082 U.S.A.
651-430-2210, fax 651-430-2211
books@voyageurpress.com
www.voyageurpress.com

Educators, fundraisers, premium and gift buyers, publicists, and marketing managers: Looking for creative products and new sales ideas? Voyageur Press books are available at special discounts when purchased in quantities, and special editions can be created to your specifications. For details contact the marketing department at 800-888-9653.

Table of Contents

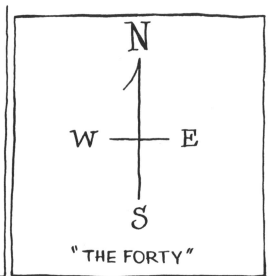

ARTLEY FARM

SINCE 1877
202 ACRES
(AS IT WAS IN THE 1930's)
LEGEND

1. HOUSE
2. BARN
3. SILO
4. CORNCRIB
5. GRANARY
6. CHICKEN HOUSE
7. HOG HOUSE
8. CATTLE SHED
9. ENGINE HOUSE
10. CALF PASTURE
11. SITE OF GRANDPA ARTLEY'S HOUSE

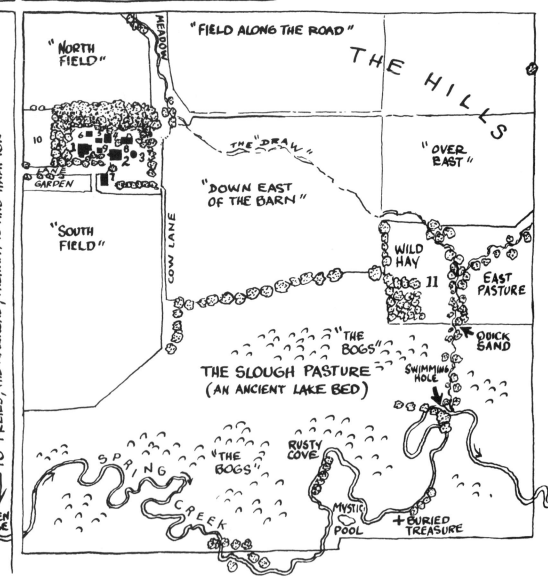

Foreword

Some of the old buildings are disappearing from the farm and neighborhood, and most of the old neighbors are gone. Little by little, evidence of a way of life I knew is fading from the scene.

When the old corn crib on our farm was finally torn down, one of the boards was saved. On it were carved the initials, G.E.B. They were cut into that pine board in 1917 by Gaines Ed Bellamy, a youth of seventeen, who after making his way from the hills of Virginia, worked for a time as a hired man for my parents. They were only a few years older than Ed, but he referred to them as his second parents.

That old corn crib board is a tangible link to that distant past. Another link is the phone call my mother receives once a month from "the old hired man" — as he refers to himself — from his native state where he and his wife, Stella, are now retired. He used to write letters regularly (before his eyes began failing) and he and Stella came to visit several times while Dad was still living. Only then did I come to know Ed. I was born in 1917, so was too young to know him when he helped on the farm.

It was a year or so after Ed left for greener pastures that I became concious of my life and surroundings on the farm. I found it good. The next few years were exciting and full for me as I — together with Dean, two years younger than I — explored the farmyard, groves, fields and creek, and became acquainted with the creatures inhabiting them.

I suppose, by today's standards, we were poor. Our house wasn't "modern" and we had very few luxuries. But I didn't know it. I felt rich. It was only in the late twenties and the thirties, a period known as the Great Depression, that I became aware of a measure of hardship.

The Depression settled down over the country like a great gray cloud, causing a gloom and a hardship that made a lasting impression on me as I entered my teen years. There were stories of bank failures and of farms and businesses lost; sometimes resulting in suicides even in our own community. There were hushed, worried conversations among the adults as they gathered on street corners, in farmyards and around dining tables. The newspapers were filled with lists of the names of those who couldn't pay their taxes. It read almost like a "Who's Who" in the Hampton area. There were foreclosures or sheriff's sales almost weekly.

At some of these sales there was even violence as desperate, frustrated farmers saw their life's work go for a cheap price on the auction block to some insurance company to satisfy demands of a mortgage.

The very word "mortgage" had a frightening connotation and I begged Dad not to ever mortgage our farm.

He turned away in silence, with a gray, faraway look in his eyes. It wasn't until many years later that I learned that the farm was indeed mortgaged even as I pleaded with him. But somehow, by scraping and scrimping and praying, our farm and our family managed to escape the trauma of a foreclosure sale.

The price of hogs dropped as low as three cents a pound and eggs, cream and beef were comparably low. To compound the problem of those years was a period of drought culminating in great dust storms that made daytime like night.

One Sunday noon we had company for dinner and had to light a kerosene lamp due to darkness caused by dirt clouds over the sun.

The drought dried up pastures and creeks (even our spring-fed creek became only a trickle) and lakes, ponds and wells. (Thankfully our well never faltered.) Peat beds in the dried up ponds caught fire and burned for weeks and months with the acrid smoke becoming an everpresent symbol of the drought as it drifted over parched pastures and withering corn fields. One fall when it came time to harvest the corn, Dad searched through the fields with team and wagon one whole day and came home with only the bottom of the wagon box covered with a few mis-shapen nubbins.

The winters seemed even more harsh than usual during those years. Grandpa and Grandma Crow were with us part of the time and were sick and suffered more than the rest of us from the cold. It was a difficult time for all of us, but especially for Mom as she worked hard at making our cold house, that was without plumbing or any of the other niceties of a "modern" house, a cozy home. Somehow Mom succeeded.

It is the life of those times and in that family farm setting which I draw upon to create the cartoon series "Memories of a Former Kid" that has appeared in the Worthington, Minn., *Daily Globe* the past few years. I was surprised and pleased at the popular acceptance of the series, even among the young. So when a friend, Jerry Raedeke, suggested soon after the beginning of the series, that I collect them into book form, and then later others echoed that sentiment, we started planning.

At first the book was to be only a collection of the cartoons. Then it was decided to add a bit of text to supplement the drawings. Once the writing was begun however, it soon became evident it would be more than just a few paragraphs, and before long the whole project started growing like weeds until our original publication schedule had to be abandoned. But even with all these words and extra time spent, still there is much that had to be left out of this book.

It is my hope that in sharing these very ordinary, everyday happenings from an ordinary family farm, that you, the reader, may be able to identify with a way of life that was good — but is no more.

Acknowledgments

To the *Worthington Daily Globe* for the use of the cartoons and drawings that first appeared in that paper; to George Kramer and the Waukee *Farmers' Scoop* for the use of drawings that first appeared in that publication; to Kristen Artley who gave so much of her time in proofreading, clipping dangling participles and doing other grammatical repairs to the raw copy of this book; to my wife Ginny and the rest of my family who have helped with this project in so many different ways for so many months; to Floyd Egner who, as editor, has served over and beyond, and to The Printers for their fine presswork, a heartfelt thank you.

the Author

Memories Of A Former Kid

CATTLE FEEDING HAS ALWAYS HAD ITS PROBLEMS — AS WE REMEMBER

4-9-74

BOBARTLEY
WORTHINGTON DAILY GLOBE

Dirt Farmer

"Dirt farmer" is a term I haven't heard lately; once it distinguished a farmer who worked the land from an absentee landlord or a gentleman farmer who had hired hands doing the work.

Dad was a dirt farmer. The name was a badge of honor as far as he was concerned. He loved the land and was very much a part of it. As my two brothers and I grew and took on the duties of farm life, we too were "of the soil" in every respect.

This was especially evident during the hot summer months when we rode the single row cultivator with its high steel wheels. If there was a breeze the dirt picked up by the wheels sprinkled over us, sticking to our sweaty bodies. If there was no breeze and the soil was dry, the dust hovered in a cloud around us. We came in from the field gritty and coated with a thin layer of top soil.

Dad was a practitioner of good soil practices before many of our neighbors as he established grass waterways and used other soil conservation measures. Mom had her own soil practices. She tried to keep it out of the house and on the farm by insisting we bathe before going to bed and scrub clean before going away.

We didn't have inside plumbing at our house until we were grown — so keeping clean was not as simple as turning a tap for hot or cold water and pulling a plug when finished. In the summer we sometimes planned ahead by pumping a washtub of water in the morning and letting it sit in the hot sun all day. At the end of the day we carried the tub full of warm water into the engine house (or milkhouse) where we took our baths. There was nothing fancy about it. Castile hard water soap was on a dish within reach and on the cement floor was a clean gunny sack to stand on as we rubbed ourselves dry with terry cloth bath towels. But we got just as clean and respectable as we do today among the chrome, porcelain and perfumed pastel surroundings of our modern bathrooms.

In the winter months our kitchen became the bathroom. After the supper dishes had been washed and put away and the family gathered around the stove in the living room, the person taking the bath placed the wash tub in front of the open oven door of the cook stove. Hot water was dipped from the reservoir on one end of the range and perhaps tempered with a dipper of cold water from the drinking water pail.

One of the problems with baths in the winter was disposing of the bath water. It wasn't much fun to have to get fully dressed after an evening bath and struggle through the door with the tub of dirty bath water to pour it into a snow bank amid clouds of steam. It's no exaggeration to say indoor plumbing was perhaps the most appreciated convenience of a modernized farm.

There were times when the dirt of dirt farming got to be a little too much. That was when the dirt became either dust in hot, windy, dry weather or mud during wet seasons. It seemed there was a lot of both. When we were up to our knees in barnyard mud, we yearned for the dust and during a drought we longed to be sloshing around in the mud. A happy medium when the soil was moist enough to stay put, but dry enough to work well, was the "impossible dream" and seemed to be a rare condition.

During World War II, when Dad was alone with the farm work, there came a time when his sense of pride in being a dirt farmer was put to the extreme test.

It was in early spring and the melting snow and spring rains had made a deep, soupy quagmire of the cowyard. Feeding silage to the cattle was a slow, exhausting chore as Dad struggled through the knee-deep muck. He carried baskets filled with silage from the silo to the feed bunks and then had to contend with the cattle jostling for postions around the bunk. His rubber boots were just tall enough to keep the sloppy mess out — if he stepped carefully.

With a basket of silage perched on one shoulder, Dad used his free arm to beat his way through the stubborn critters to the feed bunk; the inevitable finally happened! A cow, deciding to change her position to a more advantageous spot along the feed bunk, backed into Dad throwing him off balance. With his feet imbedded deep in the muck there was no way to avoid the plunge. The next moment he was sitting with the surface of that liquid barnyard up around his chest while the offending cow paused for a moment to stare at him in wonderment before going back to her meal.

Mom opened the back door to what appeared to be some kind of swamp monster. But the shock was

14

only momentary and soon she had newspapers spread for Dad to stand on while he shed every stitch of clothing down to his skin — everything except his cap which was miraculously unscathed.

Since this was during the war, the radio was on most of the time in order to keep in touch with latest developments. Along with the war news were programs to boost the sense of patriotism that was running high during those times.

Mom was preparing a warm bath for Dad as he stood shivering in the middle of the kitchen, stark-naked except for his cap, when what should blare forth from the radio but "The Star Spangled Banner." Without a moment's hesitation, Dad removed his cap, placed it over his heart, and stood at attention — a very patriotic dirt farmer through and through.

Another mark of Dad's devotion to the soil came many years later in the summer shortly before he died. The previous winter he had injured his back in a fall and was paralyzed from the waist down. I was pushing him about the farmyard in his wheelchair in what could be called a tour of inspection.

His paralyzed condition was a very bitter thing for Dad and he never quite reconciled himself to it. As we made our tour I was searching desperately for something that might lift his sagging spirits. We looked over the fence at the pigs fattening on the feeding floor. We stopped at the cowyard gate to watch some of Dad's beloved black Angus come up to the stock tank for a drink. We let a flock of ducks waddle by in front of us in their comical show of dignity. We paused to watch three young, pointed-tail kittens tumble and roll over one another in their play in the sunlight in front of the barn.

All of these very common things about the farm had always been something Dad found pleasure in. But this day, none of these things changed his mood.

As we rounded the corner of the granary we passed a farm implement parked there — a disc. Dad asked to be pushed over close to it. With his pale, thin, sick-bed hands, so foreign from the strong, work-worn farmer's hands with which we'd all become so familiar over the years, he reached out to an oil-soaked patch of soil on a grease cup. He rubbed some of the grime on his hands and with a wan smile on his pale lips, he said, "Now that's more like it — that's the way my hands should look."

I THOUGHT I'D WARNED YOU ABOUT COLD HANDS

BOB ARTLEY
WORTHINGTON DAILY GLOBE

The Cow Barn

When my thoughts wander back to growing up on the farm, the cow barn (likely as not) is the setting. There's a good reason for this — I spent a lot of time there.

I was nine or ten when I became fairly accomplished at extracting milk from a cow. And this was no easy task (why else was the milking machine invented?) — especially for a boy's hand.

Our cows, a motley herd, were not designed for easy milking. Very few had teats that were long and small enough to grasp easily, one in each hand. But invariably the cows that gave the most milk were the most stingy in releasing it. Those were the cows whose teats were extra large where they joined the udder and shorter than the fist that was to grab them. My hands continually slid off those teats. When they did, they got wet with fresh milk which made them even more slippery. A tighter grip took more energy and often made the cow uncomfortable. She would fidget and try to step away from the discomfort. Many times after a long day in school or in the fields, the muscles in my hands and arms ached to near-paralysis before the milking was done at night.

To compound the general discomfort of these conditions were the wet seasons when the cows' udders were covered with mud; or flytime — when the poor critters were covered with hungry, blood-sucking flies. And fly season was worsened by the extreme heat that usually accompanied it. Picture, if you will, a cow barn full of hot, panting cows with flies biting, tails swishing, mud-caked udders full to the bursting point, and a tired, sweat-drenched man or boy perched on a one-legged stool between two cows while trying to get clean, **white** milk into the pail clamped between his knees.

In winter there wasn't the sweat, the heat or the flies. Usually there was no mud to contend with either. But a rainy, slushy period in winter wasn't uncommon and that meant both mud and cold.

16

AND THE MILK IS SUPPOSED TO BE WHITE!

WE DIDN'T "CELEBRATE" JUNE AS DAIRY MONTH— IT WAS USUALLY RAINY AND OUR CREEK PASTURE WAS DEEP AND SOGGY.

BOB ARTLEY
6-9-77
WORTHINGTON DAILY GLOBE

Winter was relatively dry since the barnyard was frozen solid. Then, I almost looked forward to milking — as a time when I could get my cold, numbed fingers warm again. I had to be careful, though. The shock of cold hands on the cow's sensitive teats might startle an otherwise gentle creature into a violent reaction.

After going about the barns with mittened hands wrapped around the steel bail of a heavy pail of water or grasping the cold handle of a pitch fork, my hands hurt and were nearly numb from the cold. It felt good to snuggle up between the great hulks of the milk cows, to slip my mittens off and put my hands up in the warm, fur-lined "pockets" between the cow's soft flank and her full udder. Even this caused the poor creature to flinch and turn and peer at me with a large soulful eye through the slots of the stanchion.

Winter was my favorite time in the cow barn. Carrying in the silage, cleaning out the gutter and spreading fresh, clean straw for the cows' bedding were satisfying tasks. After filling the cattle bunks, we carried silage into the cowbarn for the milk cows at night. A portion was piled in the trough in front of the stanchion where each cow stood. Then silage was carried to the calf pen and to the bull in his special pen with its heavy timbered gate. The

chores usually were done early on a winter day so that at night when it was milking time all we had to do was open the door to the waiting cows and they entered — each to find its own special place at the "table."

To this day the fragrance of a clean cow barn freshly bedded with straw and with portions of sweet/sour silage at each cow's stanchion is one of my favorite delights. If ever the laboratories that synthesize flavors and perfumes should perfect the rich, warm odor of a clean barn at milking time, I'll order a large vial of it. Then when the modern hectic world seems to be pressing in on me too closely, I'll pop the stopper and sniff to my heart's content.

The cow barn was more than pleasant odors (and some not so pleasant) and physical discomfort and comfort. It also was the center of much of my learning about life.

During our milking sessions there were no motor or other mechanical noises to drown out and discourage conversation. Depending on the mood or on how tired we were, there sometimes were very learned discussions carried on among Dad, my brother Dean and me. (Dean was two years younger than I. Our third brother, Dan, was born a long ten years after I was.) We had the questions and Dad

17

had the answers. If he didn't have the answer, he speculated with us. But Dad was quite knowledgeable about a good many things. Being curious by nature himself, he not only read quite widely but observed closely the world around him. Our cow barn conversations covered a wide range of topics — from the working of an internal combustion engine to the social problems of a bashful boy on his first date.

There were many times when the semi-privacy of being between the cows (and not having to look into Dad's eyes) seemed to make it easier to discuss some of the more pressing problems of a growing boy. Maybe it was the same psychology used in the old confessional booths where the father confessor was out of sight but within hearing.

There was no sudden awareness, as I recall, to the "facts of life" for me. In fact, long before I was aware of the phrase "the birds and the bees," I was quite familiar with where pigs, calves and colts came from. And in the natural progression of farm life, it wasn't long before I learned not only where they came from but how they got to where they came from. This of course took some well placed questions — during our milking sessions. And it was by deduction that I began to get the glimmer of a thought — "if this is the way animals do it . . .." So,

back to the cow barn and a direct question to Dad, "Is that the way people do it, too?". His answer confirmed my suspicions and opened up a whole new world to me.

Years later, when I was raising my own sons, there were times when I greatly wished that we had a cow barn with some old, well-experienced cows to shield our eyes from one another and absorb with their large, practical bodies some of the jolting subjects with which fathers and sons have to deal.

Mostly, though, the barn was a quiet, peaceful place with the sound of the milk stream being squirted rhythmically into the tin pail — the sound changing from a "twing, twing, twang," to a "twash, twash." And when the pail was nearly full with a good head of foam, the sweet smelling milk finished with a whispered sound of "sush, sush, sush." There was the creaking of the wooden stanchions as the cows strained and leaned into them trying to reach for the final wisp of hay or bit of grain in their manger.

The barn cats, alerted by an inner clock system that animals seem to have, congregated near the cat dish and waited patiently for their portion of warm, fresh milk.

But the cow barn was not always a place of tranquility or learned discussions. It was also a

18

WE HAD CORN PICKING VACATION IN COUNTRY SCHOOL — AFTER A LONG, HARD DAY IN THE CORNFIELD WE COULD RELAX BY THE SOFT LIGHT OF THE KEROSENE LANTERN IN THE COWBARN.

10-11-76

BOB ARTLEY

WORTHINGTON DAILY GLOBE

place of much activity and even violence on occasion. Because of the stanchion's ability to hold the unlucky critters, the dehorning was done in the cow barn.

Old Joab Mulkins would arrive on the scene with his grim saws, ropes and pincers, all blood-splattered like himself. The frightened young heifers and steers (the latter which had already had a traumatic encounter with man's ideas of husbandry) were herded into the cow barn, a wholly unfamiliar place to them, and then enticed, guided or shoved into the stanchions which were then locked around their necks. In all their wide-eyed terror and frantic struggles they could not free themselves. With the addition of some restraining ropes and extra hands to pull on them, they were soon at the mercy of the barbaric dehorning saw that took the horn off right next to the scalp.

When my brother and I were small we made ourselves absent from the scene and tried to block out the bellowing of pain and fright of the poor critter being dehorned. Dad didn't like this either and usually had it done to calves when their horns were just "buttons," the removal of which was a minor operation. In later years there was an ointment available that when applied to the budding horns caused them to atrophy. Of course, this barbaric

practice was justified by the fact that fully developed horns were extremely dangerous — not only to people working with the animal, but also to any other critter that might be gored by them.

Quite often calves were born in the cow barn. At best these births were not without a certain amount of violence — no birth is. When a tender, struggling creature is pushed by means of an irresistable force from the warm security of its mother's womb, through a canal that is just barely large enough and into the cold, harsh exterior world where it has to gasp and breathe on its own — that's violence! And both the new calf and the mother were somewhat fatigued by the ordeal.

If we knew the birth was imminent, we piled extra clean, fresh straw about the pregnant cow and even loosened her from the stanchion so that she would have more freedom of movement and would be free to massage the steaming new calf with her strong, rough tongue, to form an intimate connection between cow and calf. If we were around at the birth, we helped the little fellow to stand on its wobbly legs and gently guided it to its first all-important meal. Usually this didn't take too much guidance as both calf and mother knew what it was all about. They had been "programmed" through eons of experience of the species. Before long, the newborn

19

was sucking and, with feeble butting, attempting to improve the flow of milk while the mother nervously turned from time to time, sniffing the nursing calf as if to reassure herself it was actually there and this all hadn't been a feverish dream. The quiet "moo" from deep within her throat was her way of saying "all is well."

But all births weren't easy. Too often, what started out appearing to be a normal birth, became complicated. It was very important that someone other than nature was in attendance then. Usually Dad was experienced enough that he could roll up his sleeves, bathe his arm in soapy water and between contractions reach in and turn a head in the right direction or search out and align a wandering foreleg and then pull the calf into a successful birth. But there were times when the veterinarian would be needed. And even with his experience and training, it sometimes was not enough to save cow and calf. Then the rendering plant truck was called. Of course, this was a financial loss. But even if it weren't, it was a sad thing to lose a member of the farm and its unborn young. The bellowing of the poor cow in her agony haunted me for days.

The cow barn was also the scene of excitement. We had a black cow once that I think had it in for the whole human race. I really don't know why Dad milked her. (This was when my brother and I were too young to help milk.) I think his reason might have been somewhat akin to that of a rodeo bulldogger — she presented a challenge. He had a pair of leather straps that he fastened carefully around her rear legs right below the hocks. With these on, the cow could not lift a leg to kick as her legs were fastened together. But when Dad sat on his milk stool beside her and reached for her teats, she attempted to strike out at him anyway. Since she couldn't lift her one leg, she hopped around lifting both hind feet together. This went on for awhile until she tired. Then Dad milked her without incident. This routine occured at each milking, and apparently she gave a fair amount of milk to make the ordeal worthwhile.

But one night the work in the fields was late, supper was late and the milking was even later. Dean and I had already gone to bed when suddenly there was a great commotion coming from the cow barn. We could hear Dad's voice, then a "whack, whack," and a cow bellow. Fascinated, we went to the window to see what was taking place. We saw the light from the open cow barn door, but nothing inside. Suddenly Mom appeared out of the darkness in the light of the open door. We could hear her voice and then Dad said something. Finally, Mom turned rather stiffly and came back to the house. After that things quieted down and we became sleepy.

It wasn't until years later that we heard the full story — much to our amusement. It seems that the mean black cow had behaved as expected when Dad sat down to milk her. But the straps were getting old and finally had had too much strain put on them. They broke and suddenly that lethal hind leg was thrust out in full force, struck Dad and knocked him and a nearly full pail of milk into an unclean gutter. Dad was really a gentle man, quite slow to anger. But this was the final assault of a day that hadn't gone well. An old broom was leaning against the barn wall. When Mom appeared at the barn door she found Dad applying the splintering broom handle to the back of that perverse critter in no gentle manner. She asked him to stop chastising the cow and Dad suggested that Mom go back and tend to things in the house and he'd tend to things in the barn.

That was the end of that cow's dairy career. She was transferred to the feed lot and became a nice fat beef type. Eventually she left the farm and was never heard of again.

Our milk cows all had names — none of them fancy — but usually quite descriptive and with meaning. There were times, of course, when their names would be changed — added to, so to speak, to fit the occasion. There was Jimima, who got her name from the fact that she was an orphan and grew up in a horse stall next to Old Jim, and seemed to have a strong attachment to him. We said she must have thought "Jim my ma." There was Stub, who had lost her tail to a beef-eating pig when she was a newborn calf and was rescued just in time. There was Blacky, Browny, and Hardy — she was hard to milk, and White Bell had a white belly and Stupid was just that.

THE FIRST HONKERS OF THE SEASON

When more cows were milked, especially after the calving season in the spring, the milking chore became more of a burden. After the grass was in good shape in the creek pasture, the cattle were turned out of the muddy barnyard where they'd been confined all winter. This meant an extra chore was added. We had to go after the milk cows every evening and take them back to pasture each morning after the milking. This was a chore I usually enjoyed — especially when the weather was nice. It gave me time to dream, to observe the continuous display of nature around us, explore a bit of our slough pasture or, in season, take a quick dip in the creek. The cows usually were placid animals not much interested in hurrying, which fit my nature — unless our family was planning to go away for the evening. In that case the slow pace of the cows was an aggravation and I'd resort to tail-twisting, stick-prodding and various verbal encouragements to increase their speed.

We got our first radio (battery-operated) in the late twenties. It was quite an event in our otherwise insular life. The popular songs were much on our mind and many of our milking sessions were a sort of concert with Dad joining in as we'd sing or whistle "Springtime in the Rockies," "Happy Days are Here Again," "Tiptoe Through the Tulips" and

several other current tunes of the time.

It wasn't until years later, after electricity had come to the farm, that an old radio found its place among the dusty cobwebs on a makeshift shelf in the cow barn. Someone had said that cows gave more milk with music. This was a concession to progress. I still think our do-it-yourself music was better — at least it was more fun.

And speaking of progress, after the boys had grown to men and the man had grown older, there came the great day when a milking machine was installed in the old cow barn. Long before that, the old kerosene lantern had been replaced by electric lights. There was a minimum of physical change to the old cow barn, but the atmosphere was changed quite drastically. For one thing there was the machine noise — the compressor that made the suction that mechanically stroked the teats and sucked the milk into the attached sealed pails. This was a much cleaner and easier way of getting milk from a cow. And it is said cows give more milk from the uniform, rhthymic tugging of the machine over the variations of the human touch. But something was gone from the old cow barn that never returned. I guess maybe it was that human touch — that man-animal relationship that has more and more gone out of farming.

BOYS! HERE COMES DAD INTO SUPPER AND YOU HAVEN'T DONE YOUR CHORES YET!

PROGRAM'S OVER — WE'RE GOIN' NOW

WHEN WE GOT OUR FIRST RADIO THE WORLD CAME INTO OUR LIVES — AND THINGS WERE NEVER THE SAME EVER AGAIN.

JACK ARMSTRONG THE ALL AMERICAN BOY!

AN' WE GOT TO WAIT 'TILL TOMORROW NIGHT TO SEE HOW HE GETS OUT OF THAT SITUATION

BOB ARTLEY

3-7-77 WORTHINGTON DAILY GLOBE

Chores

For many years the word "chores" had a specific meaning to me — all to do with the repetitious work done morning and night around the farmyard. Chores consisted of feeding and watering the chickens and gathering eggs, throwing forks full of clover or timothy hay down from the haymow and stuffing it into the horse's mangers, giving each horse a carefully measured portion of oats according to whether he was working or standing idle in the stall, and carrying baskets filled with ear corn on our little wooden wagon from the corncrib to the hog pen where we'd throw the ears one at a time to the hungry, snorting hogs on the other side of the fence. As we grew, so did our chores. We had to climb the ladder into the silo and throw down one hundred, or whatever, scoops of silage in proportion to how many cattle we were feeding. In subzero weather this job was especially difficult because the silage had frozen against the walls. Then, we had to use a pick as well as a tined scoop. After the re-

quired number of scoops of the fragrant silage were thrown down the chute into the silo house, we carried it in baskets to the bunks. This was a job that required not only stamina, as the silage was heavy, but alertness. The cattle didn't have good table manners and it took fancy footwork to keep from getting shoved or trampled as they crowded in to get their meal. In the winter when the ground was frozen it was difficult enough, but when the early spring thaws came and the cattleyard was a sea of soupy muck, the task became downright hazardous — as Dad proved the hard way years later.

Feeding the livestock was one of the pleasures of farming for me. I liked to watch pigs go at an ear of corn, chomping on them much like we do roasting ears, or see a cow eating an ear of corn by taking the whole ear in her mouth and then shelling the kernels off as she rotated the ear in her jaws. Chickens and turkeys ate corn with great relish too; I wondered how they could enjoy it since they swallowed each

kernel whole, obviously without benefit of its flavor. Sheep ate like someone at a fancy dinner, seemingly concerned with what others might think of their manners as they nibbled and then quickly glanced around.

After the silage had been carried to the barn in readiness for the nighttime milking, we had to clean the cow barn gutter by throwing forkfuls of the heavy manure mixed with straw onto the pile out back of the barn. Clean, fresh straw was then thrown down from the straw loft and spread where the milk cows would stand or lay at night with their heads locked in the stanchions.

Milking was the big chore much of the year. In wintertime our milking chore was at its lightest, sometimes only one cow. At such times we did not use our cream separator but strained the milk through muslin cloth into stone crocks in the kitchen. It was allowed to set on shelves in the cellarway until the cream came to the top and could be skimmed off and put into a separate container for use at the table or churned into butter.

When I was quite small, churning butter was done in a large barrel churn that was turned by a crank. My mother made the butter into neat, one-pound patties, wrapped them in waxed paper and took them to the grocery stores where they, along with

eggs, were traded for groceries such as coffee, flour, salt, spices and all the other things we didn't produce on the farm.

When we milked a number of cows, we carried the fresh, warm milk, capped with white foam, in pails from the cow barn and ran it through the cream separator.

In the winter, to keep it from freezing, the separator stood in the corner of the cellar under our house. But in the summer months it shared space in the "engine house" with the gasoline engine that pumped our water, a laundry stove fueled with corn cobs or coal, a hand-operated washing machine and various garden tools, empty bee hives, etc. This separator was powered by a large, hand-operated crank. It took several turns of the crank to get the speed of the centrifugal bowl built up to where the spigot could be turned allowing the milk to flow from the milk supply tank at the top of the separator into the center of the spinning bowl. This bowl housed many cupped, thin, metal discs through which the milk was forced with such speed that it broke into tiny particles. This allowed the butterfat, which was lighter than the rest of the milk, to rise to the top of the bowl and flow out of a spout in a small but rich stream into a separate container. The skimmed milk, with its light bluish cast, came out

23

another spout in a much greater quantity and was caught in larger pails.

The most tedious task connected with the cream separator was the daily washing of all the intricate parts through which the milk and cream passed. This was very important in order to keep everything clean so our cream would be of top quality. This task, perhaps because it seemed related to dishwashing, fell to Mom. I can still see her carefully washing, rinsing, and placing on a rack to dry each of the forty some discs that must be kept in the right numerical order. When older, we boys shared in this tedious task and each kept a careful account of when it was the other's turn.

After the cream had cooled to room temperature, it was poured into the covered cream can that was semi-floating like a metal iceberg, its bulk beneath the surface, in the cooling tank of water in a dark corner of the milkhouse portion of the "engine house."

Twice a week, during the summer, we took the accumulated cream to the creamery in Latimer. "Cream days" (Monday and Friday) were special to us kids. The trip usually meant a side visit to Dohrman's General Store for some supplies and perhaps a stop at the cafe for an ice cream cone. Sometimes on a rainy day when we didn't have to

hurry to return to the fields, the trip included a visit to the lumberyard for some fencing or a few boards for a barnyard gate. How I enjoyed those great stacks of good-smelling, white pine boards, yellow pine and fir timbers and cedar posts! Sometimes we even stopped at Kolb's Hardware, and while Dad was buying some fence staples or other hardware items, Dean and I looked over the shiny tools, coaster wagons and bicycles that were on display there. It was there that we sometimes got empty boxes in which window glass had been shipped. These boxes furnished the lumber for the small barns and other farm buildings we built.

But probably the most interesting part of the trip was the creamery — the main purpose of our being there. As we drove up to the loading platform beneath the canopy of the red-brick creamery, Mr. Carlson, the buttermaker, greeted us, helped unload our cream cans from where they'd been securely strapped in the trunk of our Model T coupe, and carried them through the screen door to the scales inside. Then with a long-handled dipper, he stirred the cream in each can and removed a small sample for the butterfat test. It was this test, together with the weight of the cream, that determined what we were paid for our work with the milk cows. The cream check plus the egg check was the cash we

lived on from week to week. The money from the sale of hogs, cattle or occasionally some grain or hay, went mostly to pay bank notes and interest, taxes, insurance premiums, veterinary or doctor bills or for a capital investment such as some farm machinery or breeding stock. Dad always wanted a new manure spreader but was never able to afford one — he rebuilt old ones into good-working, if not shiny, new ones. There never was a check big enough to allow for that luxury.

The creamery was a clean, milky smelling place containing shiny metal vats, wooden butter tubs and two large wooden butter churns powered by electric motors. After the cream had been weighed and tested, it was poured through a metal strainer into a large vat which held several hundred gallons of cream and was stored there until ready for churning. After churning, the butter was paddled into wooden tubs and placed in a cooler to harden. I liked to watch the buttermaker take a huge, square tub of butter from the cooler and with a grid of brass wires cut out several one-pound cakes with one stroke and then deftly wrap them in the paper they'd be in at the grocery store. We took a pound or so of this butter to use at home as part of our pay for the cream.

There was little waste with any of the products of milking. Everything had a use, even if its cash value was not great. While still warm, some of the skimmed milk was fed to weaned calves in the barn. This chore could be very trying. Getting a freshly weaned calf, that had been getting his meal from his mother's warm, yielding udder, to drink from a pail was quite a feat. His natural inclination to suck on a teat didn't transfer easily to getting milk out of a pail. The most successful method was to let the hungry little creature grasp two fingers of my hand. While he vigorously sucked on my fingers, I lowered my hand into the milk, giving him a taste of his dinner. After this worked for a few moments, I gradually removed my hand hoping he'd continue to suck and realize he didn't need my fingers to drink. This learning process sometimes took several sessions and usually was a messy job amid sputtering and splashing and assorted gymnastics of the lively little calf. Even after the calves had learned to drink from the buckets, it still was not a job I'd do in my Sunday clothes. Much shoving and splashing took place. Calves seemed to feel a bucket should be treated to a periodic butt of the head much as their mother's udders were.

The skimmed milk that wasn't fed to the calves went into the swill barrel where it soured, was mixed with ground oats, linseed meal and water and was fed to the pigs in troughs. This too was a messy, frustrating job as I tried to pour the thick swill into the hog trough while a dozen or so half-grown pigs shoved and fought each other to be the first to get the delicious mixture. As a result, the first pailful or so ended up all over two or three pigs as I tried to pour it between them into the trough.

Dad once rigged up an ingenious contraption that pretty well took care of that problem. He made a wooden chute about eight or ten inches square and about three feet tall that was attached to the end of the hog trough just over the fence and next to the swill barrel. At the top of this chute he fastened a tin bucket with its bottom knocked out. This served as a tall funnel into which the swill could be poured without interference from the greedy hogs.

There was work around the barns that was not routine so could not be classified as chores. Some of this I didn't mind, but almost everything connected with the hog house was not to my liking. I didn't mind cleaning the calf pen or hauling manure from the cow yard, but cleaning the hog house was one of the worst tasks on the farm. If the manure was moist, the stench was terrible. But if it was dry, the dust was suffocating.

After we cleaned the hog house we took an old sprinkling can, poured in about a cup or so of McKesson's stock dip and filled the rest of the can with water. With this strong-smelling mixture (not better smelling, but different than the smell of the hog manure) we sprinkled the floors and corners and lower portions of the side walls to disinfect the place and supposedly make it healthier for the pigs. Clean, fresh straw was then scattered about and the hogs were allowed to come back inside. They seemed to appreciate their clean quarters and sometimes ran around in the straw in play.

Another hog house job I despised was ringing pigs. Before the young pigs were turned out to pasture we put copper rings in their noses to keep them from rooting up the pasture. This was a dirty, dusty, muscle-aching job. It also was noisy as the pigs squealed bloody murder — not just when the ring was clipped into the end of their snout, but as soon as we grabbed their agile, muscular bodies. And the longer the job was put off, the bigger the pigs were and the harder they were to wrestle.

The job I hated most in the entire farming operation was castrating pigs. Everything difficult about ringing pigs applied here with the addition of the unpleasantness of the operation itself. Dad always did the cutting. But even to hold the screaming, struggling pig with his rear legs spread for Dad to perform the operation was altogether too close an involvement for me. In view of the empathy I had for the victim, I'd much rather have been at the far side of the farm.

There was another despised — but essential — job connected with hogs. During the cold months of the year the butchering was done for our meat supply. Usually this was done once in early winter and again in late winter for the year's supply of hams, bacon, sausage, and pickled pigs' feet. Quite often it was on a work exchange basis with a neighbor. But usually Grandpa and Grandma were on hand to lend their experienced hands and expertise in the preparation and preservation of the meat.

I liked meat as well as anyone and certainly ate my share of fresh tenderloin and the delicious brown gravy Mom made with it, but I wanted no part of the butchering process — the killing end of it at least.

When the hog was led from its pen to its place of doom beneath the old crabapple tree behind the corn crib and stuck and bled, I was far away with my hands over my ears trying to blot out the squeals of the terror-stricken pig. I only showed up later when the lifeless carcass was being rhythmically lowered by block and tackle in and out of the barrel of scalding water prior to being scraped clean of its hair. To watch the skilled hands wield the butcher knives eviscerating the animal and then remove the head and feet was a fascinating, if grisly, sight. I was struck with the viciousness of otherwise tender, loving people when it came to procuring meat for the table.

With the exception of butchering chickens, at which I became fairly proficient, I never had to help with butchering hogs or cattle. Fortunately, for me, by the time I became old enough to help with that gruesome task the cold storage locker system had come into vogue. The locker operator, who was also a butcher, came to the farm and picked up the pig or steer we had marked for our meat supply and hauled it off to his place of business. There it was slaughtered and the meat processed and put into our rented cold storage locker. The next time I saw the critter it was in the form of a neatly wrapped and labeled package of meat.

The one time I found the hog house pleasant and interesting was at farrowing time. It was cleaned for such occasions. The neat, straw-lined farrowing pens were filled with rows of pink-skinned little porkers lined up along side their reclining mothers. Each piglet tugged on a nipple, with the sow occasionally talking to them all in low grunts. It was a picture of order and security.

It was in the hog house at farrowing time that I first experienced the miracle of birth. I peered in wide-eyed wonder through the slots of the pen as one little pig after another emerged, struggled free of its membranous wrapping and made its way on wobbly, untried legs to its first meal.

Feeding and watering the chickens and gathering eggs were some of the first chores with which we were entrusted, but ones which we never seemed to outgrow. Our Plymouth Rock chickens were not confined, except in the winter, and had the run of the farm where they foraged for spilled grain, green grass, bugs and insects of all kinds. But we still had to scatter oats and corn for them morning and night. As we called, "chick, chick, chick," they came running from every direction to gobble up the grain, each trying to out-gobble the others.

Because the chickens had the run of the farm, they "stole" their nests all over. Gathering eggs was like an Easter egg hunt every day. We looked in all the out-of-the-way places — under the corn crib, in the hay mow, back of the binder in the shed, as well as in the nest boxes provided in the hen house. To find a new nest hidden somewhere was a bonanza as long as the eggs weren't too old. Those eggs were cash. But occasionally, especially in hot weather, a newly-discovered nest was apt to have eggs in it that had been accumulating for some time and were anything but fresh. If I was in doubt about the quality I'd shake it next to my ear. If I could hear it splash within the shell, I pitched it against a tree where it likely popped like a small hand grenade and released one of the foulest smells I know.

Mom occasionally made us eggnog with fresh eggs using a recipe with spices and milk. We thought it very tasty and Mom thought it very healthful for us. But Grandpa would never drink any. He explained that when he was a boy he considered it a delicacy to occasionally take an egg fresh from the nest, break open its tip end and suck out the insides. But one time he carelessly chose a rotten egg from a nest. That ended his egg-sucking days and his telling of it spoiled our appetite for eggnog.

Our chores were by no means limited to the barn and farmyard. There were house chores that needed doing too and, since we had no sisters, we boys were expected to carry a portion of the work to help lighten Mom's load.

These tasks included filling the kerosene lamps, emptying the chamber pots, carrying out the swill pail (dish water, etc.), carrying in water for the reservoir on the back of the stove and for drinking, and carrying in wood and coal and corncobs for the cookstove and heating stove. In the summer we scrubbed the privy with an old broom dipped in a bucket of lye water. We also helped with the laundry, usually working the old clothes stomper or the hand-operated washing machine. We also turned the crank on the clothes wringer. In winter this was done in the kitchen which was all steamy from the clothes boiler on the stove. For some reason, wash day usually meant a boiled dinner of cabbage, potatoes and ham. To this day the smell of cabbage cooking conjures up wash day in my mind.

In the summer when the weather was nice we set up our laundry tubs and wringer in the side yard. And while "stomping" the dirt out of the clothes in the suds tub and then turning the crank on the wringer as Mom fed them through to the rinse tub, we visited about many things. These pleasant sessions were conducted in the deep green grass beneath the fragrant spruce tree with its green, sticky cones hanging from the boughs above our heads. The sky often was deep blue and dotted with fleecy white clouds while a light breeze kept us comfortably cool.

The wash day visits with Mom explored some of my dreams of being an artist. The talks also were occasion for discussing books we had read and the philosophy of life in general. Before I knew it, on such days with in-depth conversation, the last pair of blue denim overalls had been cranked through the wringer (the overalls were always at the end of the wash) and it was time to empty the wash water onto the nasturtiums.

WE HAD TO LET THE HORSES REST — NEAR A SHADY, GRASSY SPOT.

BOB ARTLEY

6-7-74

WORTHINGTON DAILY GLOBE

Creatures

A family friend once made the remark that all the animals on the Artley farm died of old age. This of course wasn't quite true — after all we raised pigs for market as well as cattle, sheep, chickens and turkeys. But it was true that a lot of the animals on our farm were rescued from commercial enterprise to become pets, and in fact **did** die of old age.

The horses were the most important animals on the farm. They were almost part of the family. It is no exaggeration to call them partners in the farming operation. In all the years I can remember, until the time when horses were no longer used on our farm (after World War II), only one horse was sold. Colts were born and grew up to face either sickness or retirement. The one horse that was sold was actually a trade-in on a Fordson tractor — the first tractor on the farm. And it was a sad day as we watched Turvey being led away — never to be a part of our farm again.

Turvey was part of a team; Topsy and Turvey.

Topsy died leaving Turvey to be used in odd horse hitches. So in a way he was surplus.

At one time there were stalls for 12 horses in our barn. I recall the names of 11 of them. Doc was a white Arabian pony who often pulled kids around the farm in the pony-cart. Maud was a motherly old brood mare and the mother of Jack (a teammate of Jill) Jack and Jill were two spirited blacks that added dash to the simplest farm operation. Jack had a white backwards "J" on his face. Jill also was black with a white splash on her face. They both had white feet and fetlocks. Jack died at the height of his useful life when he slipped on ice while pulling a load of straw. He broke a blood vessel and died within minutes from internal hemorraging. Jill seemed lost without her partner but lived the rest of her life on the farm, helping where needed.

Old Jim was the patriarch of the horse barn. He was old and crochety when I knew him and definitely showed his favorites among men and beasts. He

29

took advantage of the men on the farm at every chance, but was very gentle with my mother who handled him without fear. Most of the other horses were in mortal terror of his teeth and hooves and he delighted in scaring the calves through fences. His partner, old Queen — the mother of several colts, died when I was too young to remember.

Dick was an old bay coachhorse or driving horse. He was much loved by everyone. Before my parents had a car, he took them to town on shopping and social trips. He trotted between the shaves of the buggy, apparently proud of his special station which he illustrated by the dignified way he carried his tail and head. Dick also had a feeling for the oppressed as evidenced in the way he interceded for Doc when old Jim attacked him. As Jim dove for the terrified pony, Dick deftly put himself between Doc and Jim thus allowing Doc to escape.

Two "blue" roans, Dolly and Daisy, were the darlings of the farm. Actually they were a dappled blue-grey, well-matched team. They were gentle, steady and everything one wanted in farm horses. At threshing time when Dad, in fresh clean shirt, overalls, and straw hat, drove off with that handsome team hitched to a bundle rack to exchange work at the neighbors, we felt a great sense of pride.

It was a fine April day with fleecy white clouds in a deep blue sky when a near tragedy put Dolly out of the work force for one whole season. Dad put a four horse team consisting of Dolly & Daisy and Jim & Maud on the disc to get some corn ground ready. A fresh breeze fragrant with tender growth and freshly turned soil blew from the southwest. The song of the meadowlark and the call of the killdeer could easily be heard above the muffled tread of the horses' hooves in the soft, yielding earth. The only other noises were the creaking of the harness and the occasional grating of small stones and pebbles against the steel discs as they turned in the soft, sunwarmed soil. Suddenly Dolly stopped pulling and stood still, her whole frame shuddering. Before Dad could act, she reared and backed into the disc. In the

next instant the convulsing horse sprawled backward over the frame of the disc with her feet flailing the air. The other horses were in a near panic and Dad desperately tried to cut the stricken horse free of her harness with his jacknife, while at the same time calming the others to keep them from bolting.

By the time a neighbor in a field nearby hurried to Dad's assistance, he somehow had brought things under control. "I thought sure she would cut open her belly and spill out her guts on those sharp discs," the neighbor said as he came puffing up to Dad's side.

"So did I," Dad said as he mopped his brow and eyed the bent frame of the disc.

Dolly, sick and very shaken, was on her feet again, trembling and obviously not fit for work. The veterinarian was called to examine the sick horse. His explanation was that Dolly had suffered from what was called the "blind staggers" — something like epilepsy. Dad blamed himself for working her too hard after the comparatively inactive winter months. But anyone who knew Dad knew he was a gentle master who put the welfare of his livestock — especially his horses — above convenience or financial gain.

Dolly didn't do a lick of work the rest of that season but spent the summer in rest and recuperation with the cattle in the lush creek pasture. She lived to provide many healthy work years beside her teammate Daisy (who died from a bowel obstruction during the summer of '36). Dolly outlived Daisy and saw her 30th birthday.

Dolly was the last horse survivor on the farm. About ten years after the death of Daisy, she fell on the ice when being led from her "retirement" stall for a drink from the water tank. Try as we might we could not get her back on her feet. She was too old and too feeble. So Dad assumed the responsibility and pressed a .22 caliber revolver against her skull. With a final gentle word to his old partner, he squeezed the trigger, thus ending the horse era on the Artley farm.

There also were other animals and fowls that from time to time found special favor and died in "retirement" or illness. Once we had a pet turkey. We raised her from an egg, but I can't remember the circumstances that set her apart from the rest of the flock. Her name was Tamey Turk. She followed us about with her turkey talk and let us stroke her knobby head and shiny feathers. She raised a brood of young turkeys but later in life contracted some fowl malady and died beneath our bedroom window on a summer night. Upon her grave we put a granite fieldstone with her name painted on it.

Frisky was an orphaned lamb our farmer friend, Charlie, gave to us. (He's the one who made the remark about all our animals dying of old age.) The lamb joined our family in early spring. Since he had to be bottle fed and kept warm, he was put in a large cardboard box behind the kitchen stove. He soon became too big and frisky to stay in the box and frequently was found clattering around on the linoleum much to the delight of us kids. Mom felt differently about the lamb being in the house once he left the confines of his box; so we had to fix a place for him in the barn.

That cute lamb grew to be a big, pushy buck that scared visitors to the farm as he discovered what a forceful weapon his head could be.

One winter day I was sawing some stove wood with a buck (no pun intended) saw, when Frisky appeared on the scene. He was fully grown then and carried a lot of weight — literally as well as figuratively. When using a buck saw, one assumes a stooping position. As I was busily sawing through a log in front of me, I was unaware of the target I was

presenting to the buck behind me. Frisky lost no time in taking aim and before I knew what was happening, there was a thundering jolt to my rear that sent me sprawling in indignation onto the log and sawhorse in front of me. My brother happened on the scene — puzzled but amused in seeing the buck and me rolling around on the ground locked in combat. There was no way I could get even with that ornery critter with his heavy coat of wool and hard-as-rock head, other than to wrestle with him.

That episode ended with Dean and me doubled up in laughter while the buck struggled to his feet and retreated, looking back now and then as if he thought the world had gone crazy. I can't remember his end, but I'm sure it must have come peacefully in his "golden years".

In the depths of the Depression Dad gave us a runt pig that just couldn't make it on his own in the competition of the hog pen. He told us that we could raise it and have whatever it brought on the market.

For years we had dreamed and talked of having a bicycle. Here was our chance! We were practical enough to know the pig would never bring enough to get two bicycles, but we shared many things — why not a bicycle? That his name would be "Bicycle" was a forgone conclusion.

We catered to him with constant feeding, watering, and scratching of his back and belly with a corncob. We fed him ear corn and swill (consisting of ground oats, linseed meal and skim milk and water) twice a day.

Bicycle became as tame a pet as one could want. He followed us around the farmyard obviously enjoying his special treatment over the other pigs who had to stay in the pen — all of which made it harder as the time approached for us to betray him for a bicycle. But we had shared that dream for too long to let the affection for a pig defeat us.

Market day came and my brother and I learned one of the facts of life farmers have had to cope with for ages — the market price of what farmers sell is set by others. The prices of that which farmers buy are also set by others. As our pig went to market, the price must have hit bottom. We were paid three cents a pound for our Bicycle. At 250 lbs. he brought the grand price of seven dollars and fifty cents. We could not buy a bicycle for seven dollars and fifty cents, even in the Depression.

Our chickens had the run of the farm — no confinement houses such as are used today. They roamed far and wide, foraging for tidbits of spilled grain, undigested grain in the droppings of the cows, pigs and horses, and insects, worms, and tender shoots of grass.

During the early years on the farm, "settin' hens" played an important part. They were the brooders that hatched the eggs into chicks. We knew when an ordinary "laying hen" was a "settin' hen" by the way she puffed up her feathers, squawked, and pecked at us when we reached under her into her nest. There were two ways a hen that "wanted to set" was handled. She was either put upon a nest of "settin' eggs" and allowed to hatch a batch of chicks or she'd be thrown in jail — a small wire cage — and be given corn and water until she forgot the idea of wanting to be a mother.

The chosen ones, however, were taken to the empty corn crib where nests were prepared from orange crates and clean straw. Each hen was put on 10 or 12 carefully selected eggs that were assumed to be fertile — if the rooster was as good as he was

I JUST WANTED TO PET YOUR DUMB CHICK!

BEFORE WE HAD OUR BROODERHOUSE AND GOT OUR BABY CHICKS FROM A HATCHERY, RAISING CHICKENS COULD BE DOWNRIGHT EXCITING.

BOB ARTLEY

5-22-78 WORTHINGTON DAILY GLOBE

constantly saying he was with his strutting and crowing.

The old "clucks" sat on those eggs hour after hour, day after day for about twenty-one days, only getting off long enough to eat and drink and cluck and squawk at anyone or anything that seemed to threaten their nests.

It was a great day when the hatch came off. Dean and I planned to be present when the eggs were hatching and despite loud protestations of the hen, managed to watch at least some of the births. First there was the cracked egg with only the tip of the tiny beak showing. Then the wet, scrawny chick struggled and pushed and finally worked itself free of that confining egg shell. In a miraculously short time a fluffy black ball of down proclaimed its arrival with loud peeps. Meanwhile, the mother was beside herself with excitement and demanded that we keep our distance from her brood.

After the hatch, mother and chicks were moved to an individual chicken coop where they were confined until it felt like home. Then they were released during the day to wander about the farmyard while the mother, with a constant "cluck, cluck, cluck", taught the chicks the ways of the world and how to scratch for a living. At night they returned to their coop, which was secure against any night marauding skunk or raccoon. This routine continued until the chicks were grown to big, ugly, naked (without down or feathers) young birds. At this stage they strayed farther and farther from their harried mother and paid less and less attention to her clucking.

Grandpa kept bees at our place. He had as many as fourteen swarms one summer. The bees and the garden at our place as well as at those at Aunt Bertha's and Aunt Ethel's, kept him very busy during the spring and summer.

There was not only the preparation of the hives and the supers that sat on top of the hives for the honey season, but there was the exciting time when the bees would swarm.

Grandpa was somewhat limited in his activity due to rheumatism in his knees, so Dad was called in from the field or wherever when the bees swarmed. With the screened mask over his head, a saw in one hand and a long rope over his shoulder, Dad would climb to the tallest limb of the tree that the bees had chosen to bunch up on. After tying one end of the rope to the limb the swarm was hanging on, he would carefully saw it from the tree and then slowly lower it to the white bed sheet Grandpa had placed on the ground below.

At one side of the sheet was a clean empty hive all

prepared to receive the new tenants, the queen bee and her swarm. On the ground Grandpa would take over. He too had a bee mask. After the branch with the attached swarm was lowered to the ground he took hold of it and shook the buzzing mass loose onto the sheet. Then moving around behind the hive he tapped a rhythmic beat with a stick on the lid of the empty hive.

The rest of us, gathered at a discreet distance, had been watching the whole operation with great interest and even apprehension as Dad manuveured himself onto the swaying limb twenty or thirty feet in the air with attacking bees all around him. The brown mass of crawling bees on the sheet suddenly started moving toward the hive in the company of their queen. Did Grandpa's rhythmic tapping on the top of the hive have anything to do with it?

At any rate, there was a collective sigh of relief when Dad was safely back on the ground and the swarm of bees was secure in its new home.

But there were variations in this scenario that made the business of trying to capture swarming bees and put them into a hive before their scouts returned to lead them off to some hollow tree or deserted farm building, anything but boring. From the first alarm of "the bees are swarming! the bees are swarming!" when the buzzing cloud was discovered circling above the parent hive, to when the last of the swarm had entered the new hive, there was excitement and tension. And to add to the tension was the strong possibility we'd get stung if we were anywhere in the vicinity. The end of a hiving session would usually find us with a pocket knife scraping out bee stingers and daubing rubbing alcohol on the stung areas.

An account of the creatures on our farm would not be complete without mentioning Nickle, the five cent cat.

We had several cats that lived in the barn and in return helped keep the rats and mice under control. They congregated twice daily in the cow barn to lap warm milk from an old pie tin, and then went their separate ways to be seen very little until next milking time.

At least twice a year a pregnant mother cat or two stole into a far cobwebby corner under the barn eaves in th hay mow or some other secret place and deposited a nest full of furry "spittin' kittens" that we kids sought out and tried to make into pets.

Every now and then one of these barn cats emerged as a favorite and became more tame than the rest. But they always remained barn cats.

But Nickle was different. He was our first house cat. And he did not work his way up through the ranks from one of the barn cats — he was an outsider.

When he was about six, Dan, my youngest brother came home from school one night later than usual, across the clover field, lugging his books, lunch pail and a cat about half grown. As he came up to Mom at the edge of the grove where she'd come looking for him, he pleaded to be able to keep the cat. He explained that he had bought it from Lester, a neighbor and playmate. With some concern Mom asked how much he'd paid for it.

"He wants a nickle for him," Dan answered. "Isn't he nice? Please Mom, can't I keep him? I told him I'd bring the money tomorrow."

Under the circumstances, financing was arranged and Nickle was allowed to stay and became very much a part of our family as a favored house cat for many years.

We were never (as I remember) without a dog on the farm. Scamp was our first. He was a pup when I was, so I don't remember him until he was a full-grown collie. He was a worthless, thoroughly loveable dog and we got along wonderfully. He spent most of his life on three legs due to an accident when he was wandering the farm one night. He was found the next morning hanging by a broken hind leg from a barbed wire fence. No one knew how long he had hung there, but the leg was mangled beyond saving. He learned to get around very well and lived many years.

While Scamp was still living we were given a female airedale pup whom we named Frazzels. She attached herself to Dad and was in reality his dog all her days. She had one outstanding fault — she was susceptible to the wiles of every male dog that found its way to the farm and was always having pups.

We were sure she understood our language and wouldn't have been very surprised if she'd actually spoken it. One time during one of her numerous pregnancies, she found herself on the wrong side of a barn door and barked up a storm requesting to be let out. It was a half door over which she easily could have jumped when not in such a late stage of pregnancy.

Dad finally opened the door letting her out while at the same time remarking that she was getting so big she should wear a girdle. As Frazzels waddled along behind him, she turned to me and gave as sure and distinct a wink as any person might have done.

She always seemed as distressed as Dad was when she had her pups. She seemed to know that he would have to destroy some of them but never held it against him. Some of her pups, though, were saved and shared with friends and nieghbors when they were old enough.

One such pup in her last batch grew to adulthood on our farm and was quite a nice dog. We called him Pat. He and his mother would go on hunting expedi-

A SPRING RITUAL— WHEN GRANDPA TOOK TIME FROM PLANTING THE GARDEN TO MAKE US WILLOW WHISTLES.

BoBARTLEY
5-15-78 WORTHINGTON DAILY GLOBE

tions on the farm and return all tired and muddy. Then a week or so later they went again. But one time they didn't return. Several days went by and we searched everywhere without finding them. Finally one morning we arose to find that Pat had returned. He was thin, weak, stiff and bedraggled. On the top of his head and on his elbows were sores where the hair and skin had been rubbed away. Frazzels never did return.

On the east border of the farm was a twelve inch drainage tile that came out of our neighbor's farm and emptied into an open ditch which meandered about a quarter mile to the creek. During wet seasons this tile ran about half full. But much of the time it was just a trickle. Since Pat was reluctant to talk about the experience, we theorized.

No doubt the two dogs chased a rabbit or some other small animal into the open end of the tile, followed it too far in and became trapped. Since they couldn't turn around inside the tile, they either had to back their way out or keep going forward to an open intake. Depending on which of the dogs was first into the dark tunnel, Pat either backed out or crawled forward inch by inch for a mile or so to reach an opening.

Apparently Frazzels, being quite old, didn't have the strength to survive such an ordeal. Pat,

however, recovered physically but never seemed the same again. A year or so later he was killed about two miles from home when a neighbor came upon him foaming at the mouth.

The bovine population was a very important part of our farm. There was a time when our beef and milk cows were one and the same — shorthorns. Later we had a motley herd of whiteface herefords, shorthorns, black angus, holsteins, and brown swiss. We milked representatives from each breed and became familiar with their different traits. The black cattle generally had a wild nature — especially as milk cows. The brown swiss and the holsteins were probably the best in the cowbarn. Despite their large size, they tended to be docile.

I was told early in life that it was better being attacked by a bull than by a cow with a calf. One reason given was the cow's singleness of purpose in defending her calf. But perhaps the most important difference lay in the fact that a bull closes his eyes before slamming his massive head against his victim, whereas a cow keeps her eyes open and on target. The theory was that while being attacked by a bull, there is the last minute chance to sidestep the final blow, but not so with a cow.

I never experienced actual contact with bull or cow but did have some close calls. One such scare was by a neighbor's bull. Our 4-H leader, Mr. Howard, Dad and I went to a neighbor's place to pick a baby beef from a herd he'd just had shipped from the West. The neighbor wasn't home when we arrived but his wife told us where to find the herd. The three of us climbed a board gate, according to the directions we'd been given, and proceeded around the barn and silo. There we saw the herd thirty-five or forty yards away on a hill where they were feeding on hay. As we approached, we suddenly were aware of a large bull among the cows and calves. He simultaneously became aware of us! Just as suddenly he arched his neck and with a great snort and bellow, started down the hill toward us.

I have no way of knowing which one of us he had as his prime target. But suddenly I had the feeling I was too young to die. Apparently Mr. Howard felt the same, for we both started looking around for a means of escape. The nearest object was the silo which presented nothing but sheer, unclimbable sides. The wooden gate was too far away. The barn, with its doors tightly shut, was also too distant; the wire fences looked too complicated for hasty negotiating and much too frail to stop an angry bull if he had a mind to come on through.

While Mr. Howard and I were concerned with what seemed to be hopeless escape, Dad was busily employing a different tactic. As the bull started for us, Dad scooped up some pebbles from the ground in front of him and with a great shout, charged toward the bull waving his arms and throwing the pebbles at him. The bull slid to a stop and with his great neck still arched, gave a final snort and turned away to return to his herd on the hill. We too turned aside and without haste, but with as much dignity as we could muster, retreated back over the gate — determined to select the baby beef calf another time. As we drove out of the farmyard, I felt proud my Dad had shown the courage and presence of mind to out-bluff the bull. That old critter surely could have gotten at least one of us and most likely more if he'd really put his mind to it.

The inhabitants of our two hundred and two acres were by no means limited to the domesticated creatures of the barnyard and pastures. The creek, the willows along the creek, the marshes and meadows spreading in the lowlands on either side of the creek, the trees that divided the marshlands from the uplands, and then farther up to the hills and fields and fence rows — all these places on our farm were habitat to various wildlife creatures that were a continuous delight to a small boy happening upon them.

Many of the birds were migratory and heralded the season for us. Such birds included the meadowlarks, killdeer, turtledove, as well as the teel, mudhens, mallards and other water birds that frequented the secluded marshes or waters of the creek. A glimpse of a red fox with his great bushy tail nearly equal in size to the rest of him or of a white tail deer sailing over a fence or of a beautiful blue heron rising majestically with its long legs retracting under it or of the honking of a flock of Canadian geese in their great V formation — all these things were a part of our farm and they made living there a rich experience.

My parents greatly appreciated nature and were quick to point out such sights as a pair of swallows building their nest on an overhead beam in the oats bin or a covey of quail darting into a brush pile or a hummingbird feeding at dusk on the honeysuckle blossoms at the corner of the house. The ant colony working in its "city" in a corner of a meadow provided another rich learning experience. It was an ancient city by our standards as it had been there for years when I was quite small, and as far as I know, still is there.

There seemed to be an unstated but generally understood policy on our farm that we were cohabitants with the wild creatures of the fields and meadows. We could enjoy them in their wild state by observation, but they were not to be disturbed or brought into captivity. Orphaned young were an exception. One time Dad came in from the field with two baby skunks in the pocket of his barn jacket. They were very young with eyes not yet open, and could barely crawl. But their marking, even at that young age, was the distinctive white stripe on black. And when we touched their soft bodies, they raised their little tails — an ineffective gesture of their formidable power in adulthood.

Dad explained that one of the horse's hooves had broken through into the skunk's underground home, killing the mother and the other kits in the nest. We put the two survivors in the granary to make them secure against the cats and the dog. At milking time we tried unsuccessfully to get them to drink from a saucer of fresh, warm milk. Next morning they were both dead — apparently having been injured in the accident that killed the rest of the family outright.

One spring Dad, Dean and I were clearing scrub trees out of a corner of a field. We had removed several of them by chopping and by pulling with log chain and tractor when one of us noticed a bird on a nest in one of the trees. Since the tree was more or less in the midst of the clump of trees we were removing, it was impossible to continue our clearing project without disturbing the bird and her nest. Consequently our work stopped and Dad said we'd finish after the bird and her brood had left the nest. In recalling the situation, I compare it to the mostly

WE NEVER DREAMED THERE'D EVER BE SUCH A THING AS A FERTILIZER SHORTAGE!

BOB ARTLEY
WORTHINGTON DAILY GLOBE

3-13-74

ineffective demonstrations waged against a road or a building project when some fine old trees or other landmarks are involved. That bird put on an effective demonstration sitting quietly on her nest in that small tree while the other trees were crashing down all about. But that bird was lucky to be "demonstrating" against someone with the sense of values Dad had.

I would be misleading if I left the impression that all the wild creatures were looked upon benevolently. This certainly wasn't the case. As in any ecology, there are those that prey upon others, and a farmer is constantly on the defense against those creatures which have an appetite for his crops or livestock.

The prairie wolves and bears that are supposed to have been in our general area in the early days were long since gone. The marauders of our fields, granaries and barnyards were much smaller, consisting of striped gophers, pocket gophers, weasles, skunks and raccoons. Some of our neighbors accused foxes of running off with baby pigs and hawks were supposed to be depleters of chicken flocks. So these creatures, along with the rabbits that played havoc in the vegetable garden and the squirrels that stole ears of corn from the corn crib, were considered fair targets for the .12 gauge shotgun or .22 caliber rifle that stood in the corner of our kitchen

wardrobe. However, it is only fair to say such action against the supposed culprits was seldom used.

Dad did enjoy hunting, though, and would occasionally bring in a pheasant or mallard duck in season. When my brother and I were quite small we accompanied him through fields and along the creek and shared in the excitement of the hunt. But when a beautiful ring-neck pheasant or duck was brought down, the sight of that lifeless wild thing laying at our feet seemed tragic to me. I secretly wanted to see them make good their escape when they were flushed from hiding by our small hunting party. Dad recognized my sentiments on this and I never owned a rifle (with the exception of an air rifle when I was about twelve) nor ever went hunting carrying a gun. But to this day I enjoy the hunt — but only to observe, not to take.

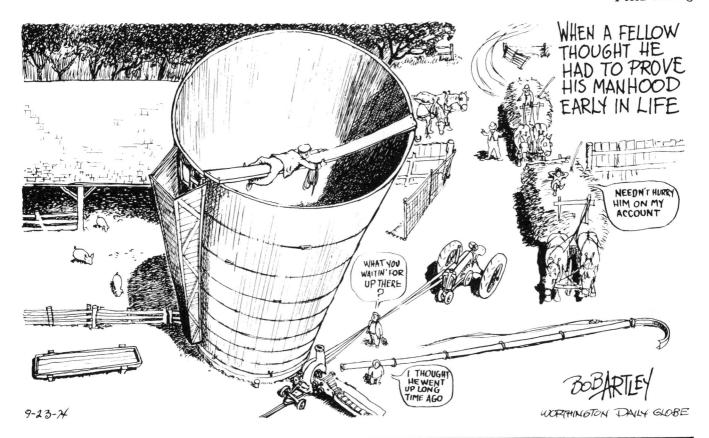

WHEN A FELLOW THOUGHT HE HAD TO PROVE HIS MANHOOD EARLY IN LIFE

NEEDN'T HURRY HIM ON MY ACCOUNT

WHAT YOU WAITIN' FOR UP THERE?

I THOUGHT HE WENT UP LONG TIME AGO

9-23-74

BOB ARTLEY

WORTHINGTON DAILY GLOBE

Field Work

Work has always been in the natural order of things for me. To be engaged in it is desireable, proper, and expected. Long before I was old enough to do a man's work, my brothers and I played at it. We played at making hay, plowing, milking, hauling manure, threshing and so forth. Our models were Dad, Grandpa, the hired men, and neighbors.

We fashioned miniature farm buildings from wooden boxes and laid out fields and farmyards. One time, Dean and I made a play manure spreader from old boards and our coaster wagon wheels. We loaded it with real manure from the horsebarn and hauled it to the strawberry patch. Since we didn't have the technical know-how to make a beater on our "spreader", I was the "beater." I vigorously raked the manure out the rear with my gloved hands as Dean pulled our diminishing load up and down the patch. Despite Mom's consternation with our method, she had to admit the strawberry crop that year was unsurpassed.

From the time we were small we looked forward to field work — as much as we anticipated becoming twenty-one when we were yet in our teens. Field work carried with it a certain badge of maturity. The older boys in the neighborhood were looked up to with respect when they first were allowed to drive the horse on the hay fork, cultivate corn or rake hay. And being water monkey for the steam engine on the threshing rig was the top aspiration of any boy.

I considered it a great accomplishment the first time I drove a team of horses by myself (even though I practically was dragged across the farmyard). With the ends of those heavy reins more than filling my hands, I took giant steps to keep up with the team. And despite my pride, it was comforting to know Dad was only a step or two behind as we headed toward the wagon to hitch up.

I liked working in the fields — usually. It was hard and there were some tasks to which I had a strong

aversion — shocking oats was one. And there were weather conditions — extreme heat, cold and wind — that made field work less than pleasant.

My first memory of working in the fields is of helping harvest potatoes on a sunny September day. There was the smell of the rich, warm earth and a faint odor of burning grass borne in on the gentle movement of air from the southwest. The breeze also brought floating cobwebs that caught on fences and weeds. Ed Mahncke, our neighbor on the south, and his aged father-in-law were helping us. They had brought several old woven willow baskets to carry the potatoes. Those large, work-worn baskets seemed very appropriate to the task. They were of the earth as were the men, on their hands and knees in the soft, warm loam, gathering in the earthy bounty that rolled from under the clattering old potato digger pulled by the two-horse team Dad was driving.

Aside from digging potatoes (and planting them), our work in the fields in our early years was limited mostly to riding along wherever possible as observers. At oat seeding time, we rode **and** worked. Our job was to keep full the hopper of the end gate seeder at the rear of the wagon. This fairly simple task involved scooping up buckets or scoop shovels of oats from the wagon box and pouring it

into the hopper while Dad drove the horses at just the right distance from the wagon tracks of the previous pass across the field. But it was all too easy to watch the whirling blades of the seeder broadcasting the seed or the drive chain turning on the sprocket inside the rear wagon wheel and not notice how fast the oats were going down in the hopper until suddenly there would be the loud rattling of an empty hopper and the whirling blades racing empty — no oats being seeded. Dad would hear the empty seeder before we did and stop the team. Then with cheeks smarting from embarrassment at having shirked our job, we worked furiously to get the hopper full again with a resolve to pay better attention.

Eventually we were allowed to do all of the field work with the exception of planting corn. This was something Dad always did. No one had a truer eye whether it was planting a straight row of corn, making a straight fence or judging the trueness of a door or window frame. So it was understood that if the corn rows were to be straight, it would be Dad that drove the team on the two-row, wire-check corn planter. That was an exacting job. The planter wires were stretched across the field. Evenly-spaced buttons on the wire tripped the planter, planting a seed. Properly done, the plants were spaced so they

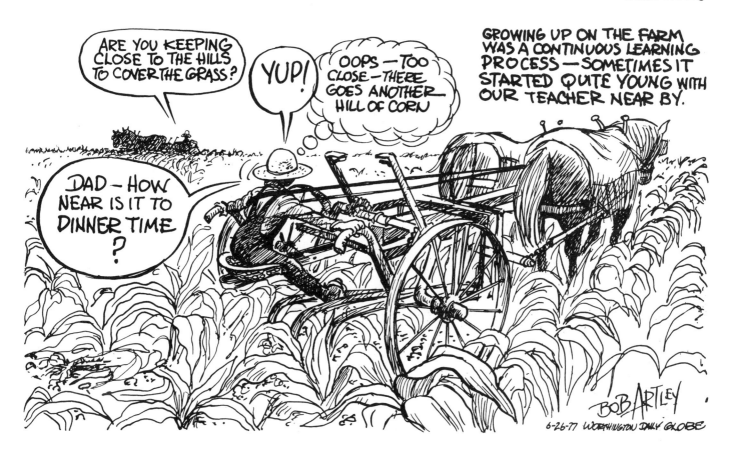

formed rows both up and down and across. In a time before chemical weed-killing, the method allowed the field to be cultivated in more than one direction.

Pulling weeds was field work too, but it didn't have the appeal of working with machinery. It wasn't grown-up kind of work. Any kid could pull weeds. And pull weeds we did from an early age. From the corn fields we'd pull cockleburs and morning glories. We usually worked in teams of two or three, counting off four rows each and walking between the two middle rows back and forth across the fields, eliminating the "enemy" as we came upon them in our rows. Late in the season when the corn was tall, the cockleburs would be too, and they were well-rooted and hard to pull. At the end of the day our hands would be calloused and stained from the green juice of the cocklebur plants with their pungent smell similar to that of a tomato plant.

Dad observed that cockleburs never seemed to be caught by an early frost. So he always saved a plant or two somewhere on the farm to watch. If the burs were well-formed and maturing early, he knew a killing frost was imminent. If the burs were late in developing he knew frost would be late. It was uncanny how accurate the cockleburs were.

We also pulled weeds out of the oat fields. Shortly before harvest time, the tall, dark-green milkweed plants would show themselves above the bright greenish-gold of the oats. We moved carefully through the standing grain, pulling and laying the tall sturdy plants on the ground between the stalks of grain. Our hands would be stained with the sour-smelling, sticky milk from the stalks and we could roll the coagulated milk into little dirty balls that felt rubbery between our fingers.

The closest we came to mechanized field work, when we were quite young, was while cultivating corn on the one-row horse-drawn cultivator. From soon after the corn was up in the latter part of May or early June until it was near the tasseling stage in mid-July, we could be found perched on the stamped iron seat of the cultivator, a loop of the horse's reins over the right shoulder, across the back and under the left arm, with both hands grasping the curved wooden handles and the feet thrust into the iron stirrup on each beam as we zigged and zagged down the row of corn. The object was to keep as close to the corn as possible without plowing it out. I'm sure Dad must have looked knowingly upon a wilted stalk of corn here and there that never quite "made it" after being transplanted.

I liked being out in the open with the warm sun on me and the breeze tugging at my clothes. There was

a great sense of freedom in walking or working my way across a field with the great expanse of sky above and the living earth beneath. The meadow larks exulting from atop a fence post, the crows protesting about something or other from the tops of the trees in the pasture or a cock pheasant sounding off from a fence row on the far edge of the farm provided some of the fringe benefits.

But work in the fields was by no means idyllic. There were times even in May when the chilled wind seemed more like January as I rode hunched up on the seat of the disc preparing corn ground. When the temperature was in the high eighties or nineties and the humidity likewise, it was extremely unpleasant riding on the cultivator with a suffocating cloud of top soil drifting along.

Making hay was my favorite field task. I liked the fragrances of that time of year. There were the early summer blooms — the wild roses in fence rows and along farm lanes, the fragrant purple clover and wild grasses and the sweet fragrance of wild grapes and chokecherry blossoms. The heavy aroma of the cut and curing clover was one of the most pleasing fragrances I've ever known. I also enjoyed the sense of accomplishment — moving all of that beautiful crop into the spaciousness of the mows in the barn — especially if it could be done without rain. And

finally, I enjoyed the physical labor. My young and growing muscles needed the challenge of strenuous work and making hay was that kind of task.

When I was fourteen or fifteen, I was deemed old enough to handle the team on the mower. I liked driving the horses as we worked our way clockwise around a gradually shrinking field of standing clover as the vibrating sickle bar felled it into a neat swath. The only thing about mowing I didn't like was the possibility of cutting into some living creature such as a hen pheasant as she huddled on her nest of olive green eggs. If I saw her soon enough, I'd stop the horses or quickly raise the sickle bar in an attempt to skip over the hen and her nest. But too often she stayed on the nest, well camouflaged in the thick foliage and flew up at the last moment. I knew if I had hit her because of the flying feathers as she sailed away. I examined the area of the nest hoping not to find a severed leg in the stubble along with the newly cut hay.

That sickle bar was a vicious instrument. There were numerous stories about horrible accidents to people as well as to animals of field and farmyard, that had inadvertently come in contact with those slicing knives. The worst was an account of a small child who lost both feet to the machine when he ran through the thick hay to meet his father.

For years we had no mechanical hay loader but loaded the hay by hand in two or three-man teams. One man was on the wagon building the load and the other one or two followed with pitchforks, throwing the cured hay onto the load from the hay cocks on the ground.

At first, Dean and I were on the ground and pitched the hay to Dad as he skillfully built a load piled high, but secure enough to survive the jolting ride to the barn. I still remember when I graduated to that responsible position and finally built a load that made it all the way to the barn without a corner or a whole end of a load sliding to the ground.

Unloading the hay into the hay mow from the wagon involved ropes and pulleys and team work (human as well as horses). About the time we were old enough to drive the horse on the hay fork, we were also old enough to work up in the dusty mow. It was hard work forking the hay back into the corners under the eaves of the barn roof. And the heat and dust of this labor sent us gasping to the open door every chance we got.

Every trip to the barn with the load of hay found us first going to the well where we quenched our thirst with deep draughts of cold water. There was nothing that tasted better to a dry, parched throat than that cold, clear water from the old, rusty cup

that hung from a magnet at the pump on that farm. Years later when I was part of a column clad in olive green on a forced march down a hot, dusty road, with only some lukewarm, chlorine-flavored liquid in my canteen to slake my thirst, I thought longingly of the pump and the rusty tin cup back home with its life-reviving water.

After the oats was cut and shocked and the corn was "laid by" — the cultivating done — it was threshing time. This was an exciting time of year, especially before we were old enough to know the hard work that went with it.

This was a time when the whole neighborhood shared work, making up a crew of several teamsters with bundle racks, one or two with wagons to haul the threshed grain from the thresher to the bins, one or two to stack straw (a mean job), the engineer on the steam engine, a water monkey (a boy driving a team on the water wagon servicing the steam engine) and one or two spikers (men with pitchforks who stayed in the field to help load the bundle wagons). Finally, there was the separator man. He was more or less the foreman of the crew and was responsible for the quality of the threshing.

The separator man adjusted the wind on the shakers, kept the bearings and moving parts of the thresher oiled and kept the blower pipe adjusted to

43

the height of the growing straw stack. That last job often led to the prank of pulling the control rope which lifted the hood of the blower pipe as it passed from one end of the stack to the other and put the full blast of the driven stream of straw, chaff and dust onto the head and shoulders of the hapless fellow on the stack.

The best part of threshing, filling silo or any work involving a crew of men, was meal time. When noon came the engineer blew the whistle on the steam engine and all work ground to a halt.

From early morning, Mom, Grandma and perhaps a neighbor lady were preparing a feast in our kitchen. Shortly before noon Dad, who was everywhere seeing to this and that, placed a bench under the apple tree in the back yard with wash basins, pails of hot and cold water, castile soap, towels, a comb and a mirror hung on the trunk of the tree for the convenience of the threshers.

The men, in sweat-streaked shirts and coated with dust and chaff, soon congregated on the grass under the apple tree and — amid much splashing, soaping and more splashing — soon had their arms, faces and necks scrubbed red and their hair combed wet and flat. Then they passed shyly through the kitchen where the women were preparing the meal, into the dining room where they took their places around the

stretched-out dining table which was loaded with the most delicious, nourishing and filling fare imaginable.

There usually was roast beef or chicken, brown gravy, mashed potatoes, steaming corn, baked beans, two or three kinds of homemade pickles, sliced homegrown tomatoes, butter, jam and jellies made from the farm patches or roadside wild bushes and vines, milk and coffee. For dessert there were likely to be deep apple or cherry pies as well as generous pieces of chocolate cake.

As the first "table" finished they left for a few minutes of talk and banter and smokes, stretched out on the grass in the yard, and the next batch or second "table" sat down to eat. When the threshing crew began to thin out, kids were served and the women also had their meal.

As I grew older and became a part of the crew going from farm to farm, mealtime became an oasis of rest and refreshment that I eagerly anticipated. After a few years of making the rounds I had a secret rating of my favorite cooks in the farm kitchens of our neighborhood.

Threshing was a communal task, but picking corn generally was solitary. The corn was picked by hand, one ear at a time. It was a job that seemed to be everlasting. It started sometimes in late

DEEP IN THE HEART OF CORN PICKING SEASON WHEN WE COULD HARDLY REMEMBER THE BEGINNING OR FORESEE THE END

DAD, DO YOU THINK WE'LL BE THROUGH BY THANKSGIVING?

NOT UNLESS WE GO FASTER'N WE'VE BEEN DOING

BOB ARTLEY

11-8-76 WORTHINGTON DAILY GLOBE

September and went on all fall, even into winter, depending on the weather. Thanksgiving time was when we aimed to be finished and felt fortunate if we were.

During my first few years in country school we had a one week "corn picking" vacation to allow older boys and girls to help with the corn harvest. After the chores were done in the morning, Dad and one or two of us boys rode the empty wagon with its "bang boards" — high on one side like wooden sails on a ship — to the edge of the corn field. The horses were headed into the downed or previously picked rows and each of us took a standing row (or two rows when we were bigger) for which we were responsible.

In the early morning there usually was frost on the tall grasses and weeds at the edge of the field and on the corn stalks themselves. As the sun climbed higher in the sky, the frost melted and evaporated. By noon the stalks and leaves were usually dry and brittle. Also by noon the barn jacket that felt none too warm at early light was draped over the side of the wagon box, and under a bright sun we were prespiring even on a nippy October day.

When the corn leaves were damp with frost or dew in the early morning they were tough and the ears were harder to break loose than later in the day when everything was crackly dry. Each of us wore a husking hook strapped to our right hand. I grabbed an ear with my left hand, pulled my right hand with its hook across the ear, tearing away the husks, and then, again with the right hand, grasped the exposed ear, broke it loose from the stalk and tossed it into the wagon.

When starting with an empty wagon the lone "thump" of the first several ears was a dismal sound. What a pleasant sight it was to see that golden yellow mound first show itself above the sides of the wagon box, piled against the bang boards. Then we knew we were nearing the time when we could climb atop the load and rest during the jolting ride back to the farmyard. The respite, however, was spoiled by the prospect of the job that lay ahead at the corn crib.

For many years we didn't have an elevator to carry the corn from the wagon into the crib, so we shoveled it off, one scoopful at a time until every ear was out of the wagon.

There were special things about handpicking corn. If the season had been good — and the yield was also — there was satisfaction in bringing in a good harvest. As with the harvest of all the crops, there was a unique, pleasant fragrance to the corn

Thus it was one October afternoon that Dad and I nearly caused Bill Freie to jump out of his skin and attack us. He was working alone in the cornfield, busily husking one ear after another and throwing them in quick succession against the bang boards. Amid the noise he was producing, he was not aware of our presence until Dad spoke. With a great shout he wheeled, hands raised and formed into fists, ready to defend himself against that which was "attacking" him.

He recognized us instantly and the "confrontation" was over before it began. Amid embarassed laughter, we all apologized and got on with whatever it was we wanted to talk to Bill about.

When the last load of corn had been picked and put in the crib — which was usually in late November — it was with a great feeling of relief and accomplishment. Except for the shocked corn fodder that was either to be shredded by machine in a neighborhood exchange of work like threshing and silo-filling or fed to the livestock from the shock, a load at a time during the winter, the harvest was done and we were in from the fields for the season and ready for winter.

harvest. And, as with the other aspects of farming with horses, it was possible to hear the natural sounds of the fields. We heard the insects and the bird calls. The wagon clunked and groaned as the horses inched it forward on command. However, the dry corn stalks and leaves rattled during the process of wrenching the ears from them, creating a curtain of sound that could drown out all others.

Doctoring

When Mentholatum or castor oil or mustard plasters or some of the other home remedies didn't seem to make an impression on whatever ailed us, Dad or Mom cranked our wall phone in the kitchen and asked the central to give them the doctor. When we were that sick the doctor came to us.

When the doctor was called, my mother set about straightening up the house, put fresh linen on the sick bed and even scrubbed the floor if she thought it needed it. If she were the one the doctor was coming to see she directed the tidying up from her sick bed — the doctor was not to see the house in a mess nor her with her hair uncombed.

No matter how sick we felt, we were fascinated by the black bag the doctor carried. Of all the instruments in the bag, the stethoscope was the most interesting, and we usually were given a chance to "listen" on it. It didn't hurt, or threaten to hurt, like his forceps, needles, and scalpels. The array of bottles and boxes of pills, syrups, and salves stashed neatly in compartments quickened the interest of all but the sickest of small boys. And though we didn't look forward to the bad tasting medicines (even those camouflaged with candy-like flavors) we enjoyed watching the doctor select a clean, empty glass bottle, fill it from a larger supply bottle, twist a bright new cork into its opening and after scribbling something on a pad, tear off a label, lick its gummed side and carefully smooth it into place on the bottle and set it on the table with the instructions that it was to be dispensed "one teaspoonful every three hours"

A doctor's visit furnished us inspiration to play doctor for several days after we were well again, using old bottles and empty pill boxes and perhaps an old purse of mom's as a medicine bag. Cold coffee served as bad tasting medicine.

Doctor A.E. Haecker took care of our family for many years, coming to our place several times, first by horse and buggy and later by car. He saw us

47

safely through several illnesses, including measles, whooping cough, broken bones, sprains and at least one serious hospitalization that was nearly fatal for my brother Dean.

I have no idea what Dr. Haecker charged for his house calls — nor how it compared to the cost of office calls we made to him in town. But I do know my parents always seemed to feel better about the sick one's condition after "Doc" had been there. And I know it had nothing to do with his compensation when Mom served him a steaming cup of coffee and a generous piece of cake before he left, perhaps to make a visit to another sick house.

Dr. Haecker looked as a country doctor should look. I remember him as of medium size with a rather generous girth. Across that girth, from one vest pocket to the other, was draped the gold chain of his watch. He slipped it out of his pocket, popped open the engraved cover with his thumb and studied it as he felt my pulse. Even though he was elderly when I knew him, he had a luxurious head of hair, black but graying, and he wore a bushy mustache. His eyes were usually crinkled behind his steel-rimmed glasses, looking as if he were about to tell a funny story, for he had an earthy sense of humor that was part of the treatment he dispensed along with the potions, pills and ointments.

The first call Dr. Haecker made to our farm — as far as I was concerned — was the day I was born.

It was a fine summer Sunday morning when, responding to the anxious, early morning call of a first-time father, he drove out by horse and buggy, examined the mother-to-be, and took off with a fishing pole for the pasture creek, leaving instructions that he was to be called when needed. He knew there was time for a few hours of fishing before the birth. I don't know what his fishing luck was that day, but I hope he had a sense of accomplishment when, with the help of my mother, a nurse and a houseful of grandparents and other relatives, he managed late that night to bring me squalling into the world.

Dr. Haecker also made a visit to the farm in October, two years later, when brother Dean was born. And of course, he made many subsequent visits over the years to keep us going.

Dean's most traumatic encounter with the doctor began one Sunday afternoon in early September when he was four years old. Our family was visiting at a friend's farm where we kids were playing in the yard with an old baby buggy wheel without its hard rubber tire. First we were rolling it, but finally I had the bright idea of throwing it into the air and then trying to catch it as it fell. On one of its returns to earth it struck brother Dean on the head, its sharp tireless rim cutting a deep gash in his scalp,

down to the skull. At first he grasped his head in both hands and danced around, half-clowning to hide his hurt in the presence of the other kids. But when the blood started oozing through his fingers and down his face, his mood changed from that of clowning to one of terror and his screams brought the adults who were soon busy trying to stop the bleeding with flour and clean dish towels. This was followed by a hurried trip to town and a pre-arranged visit (it was Sunday) to Dr. Haecker's office where he cleaned and dressed the wound. A day or two later Dean's temperature shot up and the doctor again was called. He gave him a belated shot for tetanus and ordered him to the hospital.

I don't know how long Dean was at the hospital. To me, who felt myself at fault for what had happened, it seemed days upon endless days. Mom stayed at his side constantly, night and day, as the doctor and nurses fought (without the aid of today's antibiotics) to save his life. Dad and I stayed nights in town with Grandma Artley where we'd be close by. I was taken to see him once. The sight of his swollen head, almost twice its normal size, and his eyes, just puffy slits in a distorted face, didn't seem to be the brother I knew, and was the cause of much fervor in my prayers for his recovery.

I had just begun country school a week or so before the accident, so Grandma drove me there in the morning and came after me at the end of the school day. Dad was up early with a stop at the hospital and then on to the farm to do the chores and help with the silo-filling which was going on at that time of the year.

It was a great day when we were able to bring Dean home. He was weak from his ordeal and had to remain quiet. We joked about the "hen's nest" bandage he was required to wear on his shaven head. But soon another problem emerged — he developed pneumonia, so the doctor had to visit our home again to see to his recovery from that.

The rest of the fall and winter saw Dean recuperating and building up his strength. I was so glad my brother had survived that I spent most of my time when at home inside the house playing with him, since he couldn't play outside much that winter.

There was something good that came out of my brother's ordeal, however, as far as he and I were concerned, and that was a toy peddle car my parents got for him as a get-well toy. When it came in the mail from Montgomery Ward there was great excitement. Dad assembled the little car with its red disc wheels and black hard rubber tires. It had dummy headlights with glass lenses, a front bumper, and metal fenders over the wheels. There was a dummy radiator cap ornament at the front of the curved metal hood and at the back, a windshield of celluloid with a metal frame. The steering wheel linked into a real auto-steering mechanism. Attached to the frame beside the curved seat was a realistic dummy brake lever. It was meant to run on a sidewalk, but that fall and winter the little car was peddled around the inside of the house from room to room as Dean built up his strength.

One fine day the following spring Dean and I were with Dad in the field where he was sowing oats. Dean climbed up on the seeder, lost his balance and fell off, striking his head on a piece of metal. The next moment we were hurrying toward the house with blood streaming down Dean's face from a gash on his head roughly opposite the scar of his previous wound.

This accident was harder on Dad and Mom than Dean. After another quick trip to Dr. Haecker, and with lessons gained from the previous experience, it turned out to be quite a minor thing — certainly by comparison at least — and my brother and I were soon playing as usual and Dean was living dangerously again.

I enjoyed a visit to Dr. Haecker's office more when it was Dean who was the patient. To a small boy it was at once interesting and terrifying. Saws, forceps and knives were displayed in the glass cases that lined the walls of his examining room. But it was the adjoining room which I found most interesting. It served as the doctor's pharmacy and had shelves of large bottles, boxes, and jars from which he filled perscriptions. In a shadowy corner of this long narrow room hung a human skeleton. No visit to the doctor's office was complete without at least a glimpse of this time-yellowed relic of the doctor's medical school days. And I secretly wondered how the owner of those bones would have felt to know they were hanging there in that dimly lit, medicinal smelling place.

Dad was involved in an accident one time that could have been much worse, but was bad enough as it was, measured in pain and inconvenience. He and Lawrence, a hired man, went to get a load of hay from a stack in the field late one winter afternoon. They completed the load and left for the barn. Dad was driving the horses from the top of the load of hay when he noticed his pitch fork starting to slide to the ground. With the reins in one hand he reached for the fork handle with the other. At just that moment a wheel of the wagon rolled over a frozen clod, tilting the wagon and causing Dad to lose his balance and plunge to the frozen ground head first. Instinctively he put out his hands to save his head. The impact with the iron-hard ground (there was little snow cover) shattered both wrists. When he tried to raise himself they crumpled useless beneath him.

A few minutes later, as Mom was starting supper in our lamplit kitchen and my brother and I were playing on the floor, the door burst open and the hired man helped Dad, very pale and shaking from the pain and the cold, to a chair. Dad held his helpless hands in front of himself displaying two grotesquely misshapen, discolored and swollen wrists.

Mom called Uncle Wayne, Dad's brother who lived with Grandma Artley in town, and he came out in his car to get Dad to the doctor. While we were waiting for Uncle Wayne to arrive, I took it upon myself to keep Dad company by engaging him in conversation. As he lay on the living room sofa with his deformed and swollen arms across his chest, I'm sure he must have been in great pain and fighting the effects of shock. But he tried to reassure me and answered my many questions about bones, blood vessels and the other mysterious aspects of physiology that his accident had suddenly brought to my attention.

Dad wore casts on both arms for weeks and was hampered by weakened wrists for long after that. It was probably the longest vacation from milking cows he experienced since he began milking as a small boy.

49

After Dr. Haecker retired from practice, Dr. E.D. Allen became our family physician. He too was of the old school. He made house calls and didn't seem overly impressed with his medical knowledge. Dr. Allen, like Dr. Haecker seemed more interested in the patient than his ability to pay and I'm sure wrote off many accounts. His office was very casual and had a comfortable unkept appearance. His private office contained a huge rolltop desk that was piled high with papers and books. He was sometimes found with his feet propped up on the desk, his nose buried in a current best seller. The conversation was as likely to run to books, ideas and politics as it was to the ailment you came to see him about.

It was Dr. Allen who came to our farm early one snow-covered December morning and helped my mother and a nurse deliver my youngest brother, Dan.

There were many times, mostly during the winter months when our family had the flu in its various forms. During times of sickness like this, not having inside plumbing was a real handicap. Those who were the least sick had to carry the slop jars down the frozen, snowy path to the frost-encrusted privy. And of course the cows had to be milked and the livestock fed and watered regularly whether anyone was well enough to do it or not. Sometimes a neighbor helped out or the hired man, if we had one at that time — and if he weren't sick, too.

One of our hired men, who was really not much

more than a boy, became very sick with the red measles. As Dad was building a fire in the kitchen range one cold winter morning he was startled by the sudden appearance of the hired man striding into the room in his night shirt. He siezed the kerosene can from Dad's hand and tipped it up, drinking a hearty swig from the spout. When Dad recovered from his surprise he snatched the can back and asked the obviously sick man "why in thunder" he'd done that. The hired man assured Dad it was the way they cured what ailed them back where he came from in Virginia. The funny thing is he did get well, because of or despite the kerosene, and was soon up and around doing his share of the work again.

Most of our home remedies were not that violent. However, I felt then, and still do, that castor oil was in the same category as kerosene. Even camouflaging it with cinnamon flavor didn't fool me and only served to spoil my taste for cinnamon candy. Cascara was almost as bad and was used extensively when our digestive tracts ailed. If it was a respiratory ailment we suffered, we were greased with Mentholatum from the top of our neck to our waist, front and back and then swathed in flannel rags that had been heated in the oven or by being held to the hot living room stove. In extreme cases a mustard plaster was applied. This consisted of a flannel cloth spread over with poultice made with powdered mustard, slices of onion, pepper and I'm not sure what else. The object was to ceate heat with all those ingredients. The heat was to draw out the congestion. I hated it. I felt like some kind of foul-smelling sandwich.

The doctoring on our farm was by no means confined to the inhabitants of the farm house. Dr. Schultz, from the village of Latimer, three miles west of our place, was a veterinarian who made many calls to our farm over the years, administering his healing skills and medicines to our horses, pigs, cattle and sheep.

All country doctors of that period lived hard, demanding lives as they served the sick and suffering beings — man or beast.

But the vet, by the very nature of his patient's surroundings, was subjected to much worse discomfort, working conditions and hardship than his colleague in human practice. These dedicated men literally lowered themselves to the level of the animals — into the mud and muck, if necessary — to relieve the suffering of their patients.

The Elements

A tremendous flash of white light came in our kitchen windows and for a brief moment washed out the yellow glow from the kerosene lamp on the shelf above the kerosene stove. But the lightning bolt, however close, did not cause our light to flicker nor our supper to stop cooking on the stove.

Our telephone was the only convenience that was vulnerable to lightning. Now and then, simultaneous with the great lightning flash, there was a jingle from the bells that looked like bulging eyes on top of our wall-mounted crank phone. Sometimes the jingle was accompanied by a "pop" inside the phone. Everyone stayed clear of the instrument during an electrical storm for it was said fire sometimes shot out of the mouthpiece. Whether this was true or not, the sound of thunder on a hot, sultry afternoon would bring to a close otherwise interminable phone conversations.

After a particularly severe electrical storm, Dad unscrewed the brass cap on the lightning arrester, a few inches above our wall-mounted crank phone, and with his pocket knife he scraped the contacts clean of the carbon caused by the strike. This simple procedure usually made the telephone workable again.

During the height of one storm, (one of my earliest memories of the rampaging elements) I quickly pulled a basket of clean laundry into the kitchen from the darkened dining room and closed the door after it. I was trying to make things, even the laundry, secure against the raging storm. Then I followed my mother about the kitchen as she prepared supper, trying to bury my face in the folds of her apron.

Being awakened by a storm during the night was even more frightening to me as a small boy. I was jolted to wakefulness by crashing thunder and white flashes of lightning in my upstairs bedroom. Almost before the flash had receded from the

darkened corners of the room and as thunder rolled in diminishing crescendo across the fields I scampered with terrified cries to my parents' bed where I snuggled down between the two sleepy people and pulled the covers up over my head. There I stayed until the storm moved on and all that was left of it was the rain dripping from the eaves and an occasional distant rumble.

As I grew older the wind in those summer storms became more terrifying to me than the thunder and lightning. This fear of the wind was generated one summer when a tornado passed three miles from our farm — completely obliterating one farmstead and causing much damage on several others in the vicinity. Viewing the dead and bloated cattle and pigs scattered in the fields and great balls of fencing wire and posts rolled together by the twister was sickening evidence of the wind's terrible force.

For months and even years after that too-close brush with a tornado, weathering a wind storm was a terrifying ordeal to me — much beyond the real intensity of the particular storm in progress.

Thus it was that one sultry summer Sunday afternoon a severe thunder storm terrorized my brother and me. The family had planned a picnic outing to Maine's Grove, an especially pleasant, undeveloped area with deep green grass along the banks of a broad creek and deep, shaded pools under great oak trees, hickories and towering American elms.

As the time came for us to leave for the picnic, Mom was suffering from one of the severe migraine headaches with which she was periodically plagued. Rather than spoil the picnic, it was decided Dad would take Dean and me down to our own creek in the pasture. In the spirit that half a loaf was better than none, we loaded the makings that Mom had prepared for the picnic into the trunk of the Model T Ford coupe. Then the three of us bounced along the rutted farm lanes, through the fields of tasseled corn and the oat stubble, through the wire and pole pasture gate and proceeded as far as we safely could without miring the car in the slough. With our arms loaded with the things for our outing, we picked our way through the "bogs" to the pleasant, high grassy bank under the willows — one of our favorite places along the creek.

We fished for awhile-until we tired of being teased by the minnows nibbling at our bait. We propped our poles against a tree, pulled off our clothes and joined the fish in the creek.

We spent quite some time splashing, jumping and dog-paddling in the fairly deep pool that was located in that part of the creek. Dad, too, joined in the frolic. Amid all the fun, we suddenly noticed the

darkening sky along the southern horizon. We scrambled onto the bank and dried and dressed ourselves that we might eat our lunch before the threatening storm could overtake us.

A splash drew Dad's and my attention to Dean — fully clothed — floundering in the creek pool that we'd so recently evacuated. He had been trying to rinse some mud off his feet and had slipped down the grassy bank into the creek. The next several moments were spent getting him out and dried again and into dry clothing — Dad's shirt and my overalls.

Meanwhile, the southern sky was getting blacker by the moment. Before Dad could get the fire going to roast the weiners we had impaled on sharpened willow sticks, the storm clouds had all but enveloped us. So we doused the fire and grabbed our belongings and set out across the "bogs" for the car — Dean in my overalls and Dad's shirt (several sizes too large for him), Dad without his shirt and me in my shirt and BVD's.

We had barely loaded the car and started our bumpy ride toward home when a bolt of lightning stabbed the ground about five hundred yards ahead of us. The resulting jolt seemed to almost lift us, car and all, off the ground. As we approached the grove of the farmstead, we saw a great dirty cloud rolling down the hill from the south. Just as we passed the

new straw pile at the edge of the grove, the pile seemed to explode and was smeared across our path directly behind us. Dean and I in unison let out a cry of terror. As we rounded the corn crib into the farm yard, tree branches, milk pails and great clouds of dust came sailing across the yard in front of us, all but obliterating the view of Mom standing at the kitchen door waiting for us.

Aside from the wrecked straw stack, broken trees and a minor disarrangement of the farmyard, the most severe damage was to two small boys in the form of a strengthened fear of storms.

The very next Sunday afternoon relatives visited and in our play Dean fell in the horse tank. Shortly thereafter another violent thunder storm came raging across the fields from the south, again with a lot of wind. The rest of the summer poor Dean did his best to keep from falling into water as someone had teased that the windstorms must come to dry him off.

Thunderstorms also used to come up suddenly on Saturday night when it seemed the whole county was in town. The festive atmosphere of farm and town people mingling and talking on the streets in front of the busy stores was soon changed at a sudden gust of wind and flashing of lightning. Families, and groceries, empty egg crates and cream cans

WHEN WE'D 'TAKE A 'SHOWER' AFTER A LONG, HOT DRY SPELL

7-19-74

BOB ARTLEY

WORTHINGTON DAILY GLOBE

were hurriedly collected into the cars. Then sudden darkness would envelope the town if the town's electric lines were blown down, the flow of power interrupted by the storm. The only light would be from the departing headlights and a flickering kerosene lamp in a store here and there. These feeble attempts at illumination, contrasted with the white flashes of the electrical storm, completely changed the street scene in a few moments. Farm families in their cars hurried out of town in all directions to get home and close windows and shut up the chickens.

The end of summer brought the end of violent summer storms. September days were unbeatable with the warm sun and smoky haze of the days followed by the cool nights. With the equinox came the rains — not storms, just gray rainy days at which time the prairies were soaked, and the pastures renewed for fall grazing.

The only rivals to the gentle, sunny days of September and October were the sweet days of May and June when the very atmosphere seemed pregnant with new life. The lengthening days were enjoyed to the fullest by farm kids when school was let out and it seemed that an eternity of sunny days stretched out ahead.

Anyone living on the prairies knows that strong winds need no black storm clouds to accompany them. In fact during the summer when an incessant, hot, south wind blew all day it was usually with a sunny sky. However, we generally expected to see clouds pile up on the horizon at about sundown with the evening darkness illuminated by lightning flashes of an approaching storm.

Nor do prairie winds know any season. Only the direction from which they come is seasonal. During the summer they mostly come from the south. Winter finds the prevailing winds mostly from the north or northwest. Spring is variable as is autumn, but a west wind generally is in the company of fair weather and a wind from the east is often loaded with moisture, whether snow, rain or sleet.

I had learned much about weather before we had a radio with its regular weather forecasts. And even after we got our first radio, the weather was not the big production it is in today's electronic media. We were more or less on our own in weather watching. The people of the soil, no doubt out of necessity, became fairly proficient at predicting weather through their constant "reading" of the sky and the behavior of the farm animals and the wild creatures of the fields. There were signs that told us what to expect. Some of them became part of folk knowledge, even finding their way into nursery rhymes. "The cock that crows before going to bed is sure to awake with a very wet head," or "Red sky in morning, sailor take warning. Red sky at night, sailor's delight" and "Ring around the moon, rain soon" are a few samples. Grandpa could tell when there was to be a change in the weather by the way his rheumatism hurt. A dog eating grass meant it was going to rain. Little dust devils or whirlwinds moving across a plowed field were indications of coming dry weather. Birds flying low foretold an imminent storm. A sweating water pitcher meant rain soon.

All of these signs may not have been one hundred percent accurate in predicting coming weather conditions. But I think their percentage of accuracy was nearly as good as today's more sophisticated methods.

In our part of the globe violent weather was by no means confined to the spring and summer seasons. Although at times in winter the snow fell gently and muffled the farm in a quiet beauty unique to that season, winter also had its violent storms that were longer lasting and harsher to life than were those in the warm season. Later in life I learned to fear a blizzard as I did a violent thunder storm when I was a child. (After all, lightning and thunder usually did not accompany a blizzard.) But the intense cold, the blinding, suffocating snow driven by winds of hurricane force were capable of generating their own fear. By the time I started country school I had come to fear and respect a blizzard. There were stories told of members of pioneer families who had perished in winter storms and whose bodies had not been found until the snow receded in the spring. And to walk the two miles home from school against a cold, biting wind (this before we knew of the wind chill factor) was quite an education in winter survival — to not stray too far from a warm stove.

A particular blizzard that stands out in my memory was in the late twenties when brother Dan was just a toddler at home. Dean and I went to school in the morning with no one particularly concerned about the weather as it seemed to be a mild, overcast winter day. The large coal heater in the one room school house generated more heat than we needed — especially for those whose desks were nearby.

About mid-morning, soon after recess, there was a change in the atmosphere. The overcast sky became heavier, the wind shifted to the northwest and soon the air was filled with a fine, powdery snow. It became noticeably colder. The window, which had been open a crack, was now closed and the stove once again seemed desireable. Roy and I were asked to go to the shed in back of the school house for more coal. We returned chilled to the bone

with a full coal bucket, powdery snow covering our outer clothes. By noon Miss Jamison was decidedly concerned about the developing storm outside and we were admonished to spend our lunch hour inside, except for necessary trips to the two outhouses which flanked the coal shed.

In early afternoon, when classes had resumed, Mrs. Phil Mahncke, from the farm across the road, appeared at our door with the message that the party telephone line had been buzzing with word of a blizzard. Since our school house had neither telephone nor electricity (there was none of the latter in the neighborhood then) Mrs. Mahncke relayed the phone messages from the concerned parents in the district. Those living east and northeast of the school would be picked up by Mr. Meyers. The Nelsen kids who lived about a block away were to go directly home. The Elphics who lived about a quarter mile north of the school were to be met by their father. And finally, Dean and I and our neighbor, Kenneth Freie, were to wait at Mahncke's across the road for our fathers.

All books were put away, coats, caps and overshoes were put on and the orders carried out. Dean and Kenneth and I accompanied Mrs. Mahncke to her warm kitchen where we waited apprehensively for the arrival of our rescue team. After what seemed a long time a shadowy form appeared in the farmyard. It was Dad and Mr. Freie with a team and wagon.

After our rescuers were served hot coffee and doughnuts and information and impressions of the storm were exchanged, we boys were wrapped in borrowed scarves and extra sweaters and blankets loaned by the Mahnckes, and with the help of Phil all were loaded into the wagon and we headed west into the storm and the two miles to home.

The wind was a howling gale by then and the fine snow was thick and suffocating. Dad and Mr. Freie were kept busy trying to keep the horses headed into the force of the storm, their natural tendency being to turn away from it. Dean and Kenneth and I were quite snug in our many wraps amid the straw on the bottom of the wagon box. We were covered with a horse blanket so we'd not have to breathe the frigid, snow-filled air. I pulled it aside once to look up at our fathers, caked with snow, standing against the storm. Except for them, all I could see were some faintly visible telephone wires and poles in otherwise blinding whiteness.

When we got to Freie's place we changed to our team, which was waiting in the barn, and went the rest of the way home with them pulling our bobsled. While it was only about a half mile from Freie's to our house, that portion of the trip seemed the worst. The storm was increasing in fury and the cold was

WHEN WE WERE RESCUED
BY DAD FROM OUR BLIZZARD-
ISOLATED SCHOOL —
NO RESCUE AT SEA COULD HAVE
BEEN MORE WELCOME.

BOB ARTLEY
WORTHINGTON DAILY GLOBE

12-13-76

becoming more intense. The horses were blinded by the snow and were stumbling in the deepening drifts.

Shortly before reaching our driveway where we would turn and not be facing into the storm, I glanced up from beneath my blanket at Dad. What I saw struck terror in my heart. His face was coated with snow and I thought surely it must be frozen. After the horses had been put into the barn and we had been greeted in a warm kitchen by Mom, our little brother, and the delicious smell of beef stew cooking on the stove, only then did I have a chance to see Dad's face with the ice and snow gone from it and know it was all right and not frozen stiff as I had feared.

We sat down to supper that evening in the warm glow of the kerosene lamp, knowing that the horses were safe in their stalls. And as Mom and Dad and my two brothers and I gathered around the table with a big bowl of steaming stew before us, it was very easy for me to enter into the spirit of Dad's table prayer of thanksgiving.

The blizzard howled all that night and the next day, piling high drifts in grotesque shapes all over the farmstead. We were isolated for several days, our only contact with the outside world being the telephone — if the wind didn't blown down a wire somewhere. I felt very secure in my little world and wanted nothing more.

Things of The Spirit

From childhood I was made aware of the presence in our lives of more than that which could be bought and sold and otherwise touched or held in the hands. This awareness was accentuated through a period of years known as the Great Depression.

There was love in our home during those years, and fun and laughter. Our family was blessed with a lively sense of humor that saw us through many rough or bleak situations. And we felt that God too, understood and appreciated the humor which at times showed up in our prayers.

With many years of constant use, Dad's table prayer became somewhat like a worn phonograph record. It was almost unintelligible to the rest of us as we nevertheless bowed our heads in reverence. Sometimes some of us kidded Dad about hoping God could understand. Our little brother, Dan, inquired in all seriousness why Dad asked God to bless the "district attorney"

How he had heard "district attorney" remained a family mystery. The prayer was: "Our Father who art in Heaven, guard and protect us through the day. Thank Thee for this food and bless it to our use and us to Thy service. For Christ's sake, Amen."

Being that we lived off the land we never went hungry as many did in the cities in those days. Our cows still gave milk, our hens laid eggs and we still had meat, potatoes and home-canned tomatoes, applesauce, and cherries. All were grown on the farm. And homemade jams and jellies together with home-churned butter was spread on bread that Mom baked in our kitchen range even during the worst of the Depression. The wonderful fragrance of fresh-baked bread did its part in giving our home an atmosphere of love and security as we boys came home from school.

Our clothing and other personal and household items showed the presence of the hard times. There was a time when Dean and I were near enough the same size that we shared a new pair of pants. One

OUR AIRCONDITIONING WAS QUIET, CHEAP AND NO ONE EVER COMPLAINED OF IT GETTING TOO CHILLY

7-19-77 WORTHINGTON DAILY GLOBE

Sunday morning when it was my turn to go to church wearing the one good pair of pants, Dean gave Grandma a merry laugh by lamenting the fact that he wouldn't be able to go to heaven because he would have no pants to wear.

We didn't get to Sunday school and church very often. In my early years we had no car and for much of the time were quite isolated by either mud or deep snow. Then during the Depression we were overly self-concious of patched and threadbare or outgrown clothes so tended to avoid going to places like church where nice clothes seemed important.

But not going to church didn't mean we were unmindful or neglectful of our spiritual life. We had instruction in our home of the Christian faith and a time for family worship when Mom read from the Bible, or from Hurlburt's ''Easy Steps for Little Feet''. These were stories from the Bible in language children could understand. Then all of us knelt to say the Lord's Prayer.

When Dean and I were small we sometimes vied to be the first to get up from our knees and clamber upon Dad's back in horseback fashion, grasping his overall suspenders before he had a chance to get up. Sometimes our ''horse'' would buck and there was a time of frolicking, giving relief to the previous quiet and solemnity.

We never grew tired of the Bible stories and there was discussion from time to time concerning the reading. And there was no doubt that they made an impression on us — but not always in the desired way.

One afternoon Dean came running into the house crying, obviously frightened. When Mom questioned him as to the problem he said that I was going to offer him as a sacrifice like Abraham set out to do with his son Isaac. In this case, however, no ram was needed as a substitute — Mom intervened.

Our spiritual nourishment was not confined to the Bible, however. Mom also read aloud to us from the classics. Many long winter evenings were all too short as we became acquainted with Robin Hood, portions of Shakespeare, Kidnapped, King Arthur, Treasure Island, Tennyson, Dickens and Mark Twain, to mention a few. And even during the darkest days of the Depression we were made rich in experiencing these adventures into the minds and spirit of these great authors.

When Dean and I were of confirmation age, our neighbor and mother's best friend, Virginia Allinson, drove us and her daughter Becky to the classes held one afternoon a week for several weeks at the Methodist church. When we had satisfied the required number of sessions at those classes and

59

"...TO GRANDMOTHER'S HOUSE WE GO — THE CHEVROLET KNOWS THE WAY THROUGH THE WHITE AND DRIFTED SNOOOOW..."

STEVE STEPPED IN THE PUMPKIN PIE

BOB ARTLEY

WORTHINGTON DAILY GLOBE

11-26-75

could answer a prescribed number of questions pertaining to what we had been studying, we were deemed ready to become church members.

Confirmation Sunday came. All of the confirmation candidates were lined up stiff and uncomfortable in our Sunday clothes (some having new ones) in the front pew of our large sanctuary. This day we were to become full-fledged members of the Methodist church. It was a solemn and impressive occasion. However, I can barely remember it. Certainly it wasn't what I could call a religious experience. In those several weeks of classes I didn't learn anything concerning the tenets of the Christian faith beyond what I had already learned at home. But there were some facts concerning John Wesley and the Methodist church that were added to my store of knowledge.

Tangible evidence I still have of this particular time in my life is the red letter, illustrated Holy Bible bound in soft leather that I received upon confirmation. It is badly in need of repair, after all these years, but on its fly leaf, which has come loose from the binding, is the inscription, "presented to Bob Artley by Grandmother Frances J. Artley".

The church did have an influence in my life. There were some meaningful experiences I had there. When I was in high school, our pastor, the Rev.

Cleworth, was an important person to me. He was an easy man to talk to and his sermons, as well as his private words of wisdom, were a positive force in my life.

Basically, however, my ideas of Christian living were learned at home by instruction and example of daily living. As I grew older I became aware there was a more personal aspect of my faith that I needed and I was searching for that fulfillment — a search that was to go on for many years in a constant journey of growth and discovery.

One step along this journey was taken one night at an evangelistic meeting when I was one of a few in my high school class to go "down front" and acknowledge that Christ was important in my life. I had strong, mixed feelings about this experience — I did not like the evangelist nor his flamboyant, impersonal showmanship — a feeling that has remained with me. But within me there was a feeling that I was searching to fulfill a basic need. And I knew I had made an inner friend who was to see me through many rough years ahead.

WHEN 'TWELVE DAYS OF CHRISTMAS' WASN'T VERY PROMISING

12-27-74

BOB ARTLEY

WORTHINGTON DAILY GLOBE

Christmas

When we were quite small the year seemed to be divided into two seasons — summer and Christmas. For weeks which stretched into months, there was the anticipation of and the preparation for the celebration of the great event. Many hours were spent thumbing through the pages of the Montgomery Ward or Sears Roebuck catalogs. We didn't expect to get all the things so tantilizingly illustrated in those great purveyors of the American culture, but it was fun to just look. After the catalogs were no longer current they were assigned to the privy where their tissue thin pages (roughly comparable to "squeezably soft" Charmin) were once again read with interest.

As the approach of Christmas was reduced to days instead of weeks, the tension built and it became increasingly hard to carry on our everyday existence. But somehow we managed to make it to the pinnacle of the Christmas season. The day before Christmas found the air filled not only with fragrances from Mom's kitchen (freshly baked buns, mince and pumpkin pies plus the other makings for feasting) but also with the magic of the season.

We kids thought we were especially blessed. With two sets of grandparents nearby, services at church and a celebration at home, Christmas could be enjoyed four times. After starting school, we were to add a fifth celebration.

Christmas wasn't always a time of festivity and going from celebration to celebration. Sometimes we strongly suspected Santa of carrying germs and we'd observe the joyous season propped up in bed with flannel rags soaked in mentholatum wrapped around our necks. But even my memories of that aren't all bad. There were the lighted candles at the windows and the Victrola phonograph playing "Silent Night" and other Christmas carols. And there were still the presents and being with the immediate family. It was a quiet and peaceful kind of

Christmas.

When we were older, the Christmas program at our one-room country school was the "kick-off" for the round of celebrations. We had been preparing for weeks, learning our recitations, practicing carols and working on a skit or two. One evening, shortly before the beginning of the Christmas vacation, parents, neighbors and friends were packed into the schoolhouse to admire — and perhaps endure — the talents of the upcoming generation. There in the light of the hissing gas lanterns and kerosene wall lamps we performed. After the program everyone was treated to a variety of holiday goodies from the farm kitchens of the school district. As if by miracle, the treats appeared out of boxes and baskets previously stacked in the hall and in corners.

Then the men gathered to stand in conversation groups to discuss the crops, weather and the merits and demerits of President Cal Coolidge. The women "oh'ed" and "ah'ed" over the sandwiches, cakes, cookies and pies and expressed a desire for this or that recipe. Or they commented on how cute Wilbur was when he forgot his lines and how sweet Lucille looked in her curls and pinafore, and what a marvelous job the schoolteacher Miss Jameson had done in pulling the whole thing off.

We kids stood on one foot and then the other, self-conscious in the presence of the parents of our schoolmates. I, for one, was quite pleased with what I thought was a brilliant comic performance in the skit. Until, that is, on the way home my brother Dean informed me my fly had been open.

There was one Christmas program at our school that would have been tragedy but for the cool-headed reaction of my kid brother. He and several other boys and girls were acting out a skit on the slightly raised platform that served as our stage. Part of the skit called for them to join hands and skip around the lighted Christmas tree while singing. Suddenly, in one horrible moment, the beautiful, flowing hair of the little girl in front of my brother came in contact with one of the lighted candles on the tree. In an instant a flame shot up her beautiful tresses and a gasp of horror came from the audience. Just as suddenly, and without missing a step or a note of the song, my brother gave one enormous puff and blew out the fire. The skit continued uninterrupted to its conclusion. Dean always was the hero type!

Christmas eve was the next event on the agenda of our celebration. Chores were done up early. An extra portion of grain was given to the farm animals and their stalls and pens were made a little more comfortable with additional bedding straw. By the time milking was done and the milk brought to the kitchen and strained through clean muslin cloth into large crocks, the sun was going down like a big red ball behind the rolling, snow-covered hills to the southwest of our farm. Soon we were all cleaned up and ready for our trip to Grandma Artley's in town.

During my early years we didn't have a car. We got about by horse and buggy most of the year. When the ground was snow-covered, we traveled with team and bobsled for social trips as well as for coal, groceries and other supplies. The bobsled was a farm implement, a wagon box set on runners. It didn't have the grace of a sleigh, but it functioned just as well. Even after we did have a car, it was often more convenient to use the bobsled in winter.

What is probably my earliest Christmas memory includes a bobsled ride. It was shortly after sundown when Dad carried my brother and me across the farmyard. His boots crunched in the frozen snow. He deposited us in the deep clean straw in the bottom of the wagon box. Dolly and Daisy, already hitched to the sled, gave their harness a shake and snorted clouds of frosty breath, showing their impatience to have the sled loaded and on its way. A large clothes basket filled with gaily wrapped gifts and a picnic basket with food for the potluck supper were loaded toward the back of the wagon box. A kitchen chair was put aboard for Mom and soon she and my brother and I were made snug and warm wrapped in blankets and a huge, hairy, horsehide robe. A hot soapstone, just taken from the kitchen oven was put under Mom's feet.

Dad, too, was prepared for the trip. He had on his great driving coat made of canvas and lined with the tight, curly wool of sheepskin. It extended from his ankles to a wooly collar that turned up high around his head and he wore a black wool scotch cap with ear flaps. On his hands were hairy horsehide gauntlet-type mittens which covered wool mitten liners. Thus equipped, one could drive horses through even a blizzard in reasonable comfort.

With a flip of the reins and a "click, click" with his tongue, Dad started the horses and guided them out of the farmyard and down the lane. He stood in the front of the box, occasionally stamping his feet to keep them warm.

There was not a cloud in the sky and the rosy glow of the setting sun behind the snow-covered hills had all but disappeared as we turned onto the township road past our place. Along the southwestern horizon — about where the sun had sunk from sight — was the twinkling light that shown every night of the year from atop the water tower of the village of Coulter — about three miles away. It was the only man-made light on the horizon. Not far above it in the southwest sky was the first glimmering of the evening star. Before getting to Hampton, six miles away, the whole sky would be studded with its bright winter jewelry. But now the white blanket of fresh, clean snow seemed to emit its own light. There had been no traffic past our place since the new snow earlier in the afternoon and the runners of the bobsled were the first to write their story on the clean, frosty white beneath us.

A snowy owl glided silently across the road in front of the horses and came to a perch on a telephone pole from which he watched us intently as we slid past. A pair of jackrabbits, cavorting in the snow-filled ditch at the side of the road, took off across a field with their peculiar loping gait as we drew near. The horses and sled produced a crunching rumble as they crossed the snow-covered bridge; we peered over the side to see the frozen creek beneath. Here and there were steaming holes in the ice where springs bubbled up and kept the water from freezing. There were also the fresh tracks of some small animal that had taken advantage of this frozen bridge across the water.

At the top of the hill, by our neighbor Bill Freie's home, I glanced back at the farm we'd just left — dark and silent in the distance. I knew that beneath the snow-covered roofs of the barn and sheds the animals were snug in the straw and their winter coats. In that tall, dark, silent house I knew there was a living-room stove in which the fire had been carefully banked so there would be some warmth upon our return later that night. I also knew there were some Christmas secrets tucked beneath the fragrant boughs of a tinseled tree in front of the west window and that in the morning those secrets would be discovered. I felt warm and secure and excited — it was a wonderful world!

Bill Freie had just finished milking and was on his way from the barn to the house with a pail in one hand and a kerosene lantern in the other. He raised his lantern arm in friendly greeting to Dad's "Hi, Bill" and as an afterthought called "Merry Christmas." I glanced at their lighted window and knew that Kenneth, a few years my senior, must be in their immaculate kitchen waiting for supper and their Christmas.

We crossed over the railroad tracks where the iron of the sled's runners screeched over the cold steel of the rails that stretched out into the winter darkness both east and west. Except for that screech, it was a quiet ride. There was only the muffled "clop" of the horses' hooves, the creaking and jingling of the harness (we had no sleighbells) and the quiet sound of the runners cutting through the snow or sliding over frozen ruts to break the frigid silence of the winter air.

OUR WINTER RECREATION WAS SOMETIMES BY MOONLIGHT AND INCLUDED THE ENTIRE FAMILY AS WELL AS OUR PETS — ON A LARGE HOMEMADE PONY SLED

When the air was still, it was easy to pass the time in conversation or singing if we liked. Once, on such a trip, Dad asked me to check to see if the right rear runner was sliding. Before thinking about it, I peered over the side to see that it was indeed sliding — much to Dad's amusement.

Even with all the precautions taken against the cold, by the time we got into town and pulled up in front of Grandma Artley's big, substantial house, our fingers and toes were tingling and we spent the first several minutes after our arrival getting warm over the furnace registers.

Grandma was at the door to greet us. As was her manner, she gave each one special and deliberate attention, seemingly oblivious to the hubbub around her. Her family meant a great deal to her and she seemed to be in her glory when she was in the midst of the noise and confusion that it produced.

And noise and confusion there was! It seemed each one there had something that had to be said — all at the same time. In order to be heard, each had to raise his voice much higher than the other until there was finally a hopeless cacophony. All the cousins seemed to come at us at once and my brother and I were momentarily taken aback in our shyness. But before long, we were part of the pack that went whooping and yelling through the house

releasing that pre-Christmas tension. Suddenly there was an even louder noise telling us to be quiet — and then Grandma, in her quiet dignity, announced that supper was ready.

After a royal candle-lit Christmas supper we were all once again stuffed into our sweaters, coats, boots, mittens, mufflers and caps and bundled off to the Christmas eve program at the church.

The church was decorated with pine boughs and candles at the windows. At one side of the pulpit stood the biggest, most beautifully decorated evergreen tree I had ever seen standing inside a building. Beneath it were some brightly-wrapped packages that no one ever seemed to get around to opening. (And I wondered at that.) In back of the tree in the shadowy corner were some large cardboard boxes.

The program was put on by the Sunday school department. The many classes gave various recitations having to do with Christmas — the Christ child, Bethlehem, the shepherds, wisemen, etc. Those taking part were of all ages from the lisping, almost inaudible kindergarten through the high school students who performed a costumed pageant of the birth of Jesus in the stable.

After the last piece had been spoken and the last carol had been sung, (and still no one had opened the packages under the tree) the Rev. Hurlburt gave the closing prayer. He had barely said "amen" when the sound of sleigh bells and stomping and "ho-ho-ho" suddenly came from the back of the church. And as we turned to see what was the matter, the swinging doors burst open and in came none other than Santa Claus — in boots, red suit, whiskers and all. He came down the aisle waving and calling "Merry Christmas." I was seated where he passed nearby. Thus I had a pretty good look at that famous personage. It bothered me to see that while he waved with one hand, he seemed to be using the other to hold his face on. And from the rigid expression on his face, I came to the immediate conclusion that Santa had not wrapped up in his muffler properly and had frozen his face stiff! I had heard that ears might fall off if frozen — so why not a face? And while Santa — with the help of some men from the audience — dragged out those mysterious big cardboard boxes from behind the Christmas tree and from them took little packages of candy and nuts which were distributed to all of the children present, I was pondering the awful fate that had befallen poor Santa's face.

Back at Grandma's after the church program, there was a different mood. We all gathered in the long living room which was lit only by the light of the tree (it had colored electric bulbs because private electrical power was available in Hampton) and a blazing wood fire on the hearth.

Just when things seemed comparatively calm and we kids were contemplating the pile of gifts beneath the tree, we heard the front door open and there was Santa again. Everyone seemed startled, especially cousin Johnny, about my age, who started hollering and screaming at the top of his voice and continued to do so until Santa had taken some things out of his pack and departed. I couldn't help notice how much thinner he'd become since we'd seen him at the church less than an hour before. Perhaps it was due to his rough schedule or his frozen face — which I noticed was still stiff. I also thought it a shame that Uncle Wayne, who came sauntering down the stairs a few moments later, had missed Santa's visit.

About ten o'clock everyone claimed their own gifts from among the tangle of wrappings, ribbons and kids on the floor and loaded them into their baskets along with casseroles, pie tins and cake pans. We once again were stuffed into our winter wraps and amid noisy "good nights" and "Merry Christmases" and a special "good night" and "thank you to Grandma, we left for home.

The homeward trip seemed quite short since my brother and I, wrapped snugly in blankets and robes in the straw in the bottom of the sled, were soon in deep sleep. We awoke while we were being carried into our house and remained awake only long enough to see to the hanging of our stockings.

In the meantime Dad had put the horses away and revived the fire in the stove. Mom dressed us in our cotton flannel footed pajamas beside the crackling stove fire, heard our nighttime prayers at her knee and tucked us snugly beneath the covers with a hot water bottle between us at our backs.

As I drifted off to sleep, I was glad that we'd gotten our stockings up in time to catch Santa before he got to our place. And in view of the evening's experiences I was glad I would be asleep when he made his call. I couldn't bear to think what shape poor Santa and his face would be in by then.

I was awakened by my brother shaking my shoulder and announcing "it's Christmas." The rays of the rising sun made bright our east window which was thickly coated with frost. All sleepiness immediately left me and we started speculating about whether Santa had indeed been there and done what was expected of him. There was only one way to find out. We called out to our parents whose bedroom was at the end of the hall. There was no answer but we heard them moving around downstairs and heard the stove door clank as wood was being added to the crackling fire. Then the stair door opened and Dad called to ask if we were going to sleep all day.

The warmth of the living room was a cozy contrast to the cold upstairs and my brother and I were soon spilling the contents of our stockings onto the rug. There were trinkets, candies and nuts and at the toe of the sock an enormous orange. There was just one thing wrong. In my stocking was the harmonica Dean had wanted and in his stocking was the miniature tootsie toy train I had asked for. Santa, who knew whether we'd been bad or good, couldn't keep our stockings straight. He must have been in real bad shape when he got to our house.

Our attention was turned to the tree. In addition to the mysterious packages that had been beneath it for several days was a bright red table and two red chairs Dad had made for us. The smell of fresh paint just barely dry, mingled with the fragrance of the tree, was one that became a part of the smells of Christmas. During our younger years there was hardly a Christmas that didn't include something Dad had made — a toy barn, a house, windmill and wooden train cars to go with a metal engine we had are the homemade toys I remember best.

When the presents all had been unwrapped, inspected and tried, we had a breakfast of freshly baked buns, eggs, bacon, oatmeal and hot chocolate. Then back to our presents again, among which were books for each of us.

After the morning chores were completed, we prepared for a bobsled ride to yet another

Christmas celebration. This one was at Grandpa and Grandma Crow's farm 12 miles distant.

It was noon when Dolly and Daisy pulled our sled into Grandpa's farmyard. There were a couple of cars — one a model-T Ford coupe — parked in the farmyard with driving robes draped over the radiators. Grandpa immediately appeared on the porch, buttoning his coat as he strode toward us down the freshly shoveled walk to the front houseyard gate. After helping us and our packages to the door, Grandpa helped Dad put the horses in the barn in a stall that had been made ready for them. He gave them generous portions of oats and timothy hay for their Christmas dinner.

There was always a great show of affection when Mom's family greeted one another so I was kept busy wiping kisses off my face for several moments after our arrival. But things did settle down to normal and we cousins were soon examining the fragrant Christmas tree in the parlor — at a discreet distance of course. Along with the heap of packages under the tree, there were some brightly wrapped little packages partially hidden here and there among the tinseled branches. In addition to the tinsel, the tree was decorated with chains made from brightly colored paper, strings of popcorn, some popcorn balls wrapped in waxed paper and

several paper cones filled with candy and popcorn and peanuts in the shell. At the top of the tree was a star fashioned out of cardboard and covered with foil.

Since the tree's secrets couldn't be revealed until after dinner, we went to the kitchen to see how the meal was coming. Grandma was at the helm with Mom and my aunts making the last minute preparations and carrying tumblers of milk and water, pickle trays and bowls of salad from the kitchen to the stretched out oak table in the dining room.

Grandma interrupted stirring the chicken giblet gravy to cup my chin in one hand and ask if I was hungry. I assured her I was. In fact after the long ride in the crisp winter air and in the presence of the wonderful, blended fragrance of roasting chicken, perking coffee, freshly baked rolls, pumpkin and mince pies and the faint smell of burning corn cobs from the big black cookstove — I was starved.

The slanting rays of the winter sun came through the south dining room windows of that old farmhouse as we bowed our heads while Grandpa asked the Lord's blessing on all of us and upon the food of which we were about to partake.

After dinner the women cleared the table and the men put on their coats and caps and went out to inspect the barns and Grandpa's market pigs which he

hoped to sell soon after the first of the year. We kids, having staved off starvation, could now devote our full attention to the Christmas tree and its mysterious treasures in the parlor. Just when it seemed as if we could not contain pent up excitement any longer, it was announced that now we'd "have the tree." Everyone gathered in a loose semicircle in easy chairs, rockers and straight-back dining chairs around the decorated tree with Grandma and Grandpa in the place of honor. As our oldest cousin (the one who could read) read off the names on the packages, we "illiterates" delivered them. Once the commotion of opening the presents had subsided a bit, Aunt Bertha sat down at the old upright piano and started playing carols and little by little drew most of the group into singing them.

Well before it was time to light the kerosene lamps, cold chicken, rolls, dressing and other leftovers from the dinner were put back on the table and despite protestations of still being "stuffed"

from dinner, everyone dug in heartily to a lunch that was topped off with spicy pumpkin pie with real whipped cream.

The sun had disappeared behind grey cloud banks looming up from the horizon as we were loaded into the bobsled. The air had warmed up considerably since our arrival. The pungent smell of the horses, just taken from the warm stall and hitched to the sled, was pleasant. Amid "goodbyes" from the chorus of waving arms from the farm house steps and doorway, the team drew the sled down the long maple-lined lane toward home. As I wiped the last kiss from my cheek with my coat sleeve my brother announced, "I **like** Christmas."

School

My formal schooling began when I was six years old — at home.

Our farm was between two country schools, each two miles away. Normally, in such a situation, parents were allowed to choose which school their child would attend. But we had no car at that time and the roads we lived on were mud a good share of the year, making any passage difficult. Mom had been a country school teacher before her marriage and she asked permission from Mr. Henderson, the county superintendent, to teach me my first year at home.

He agreed and every morning, from nine o'clock to noon, five days a week, school was in session in our kitchen. It wasn't easy for me or Mom in such a familiar and family-used place. I looked forward to Saturday as much as any schoolboy anywhere. My school desk again was our table, my schoolroom again the kitchen and my teacher was again my Mom. I wasn't easy to teach and balked at the regimen of textbooks and slate and tablet.

The fall I became seven we had a car and Mom had had enough of teaching school in the house. It was decided that I would enter second grade at the north school where I knew one of the pupils.

As the end of summer approached and the fateful first day of school came ever closer, I could not bear to even look at a school house, any school house, as we passed them on the road. Even having new clothes, a new lunch pail and a new wooden pencil box with its wooden ruler, pencils and eraser didn't sweeten the situation for me.

The morning of my first day I had no appetite for the breakfast Mom prepared. Dressed in my new school clothes and with tears streaming down my cheeks I pleaded to be allowed to stay home. I promised to study hard and not balk at going to school in the kitchen. That arrangement seemed pretty good to me after all.

But fate moved relentlessly on and I soon found

myself standing beside my mother being introduced to my new teacher — pretty, red-haired Miss Morgan. All the kids seemed to be old hands at this school business and gave me the impression I was an odd intruder into their tight association. Even the boy I knew previously seemed to desert me. I wanted to go home.

During the next few weeks my resistance to becoming educated wore down and gradually the daily trip to school was made with less apprehension. I began to feel accepted by the other school kids — by all except Otto, who seemed to have something against me — and he carried quite a bit of influence in the school yard. When winter came he brought his new sled to school. Everyone was permitted to play with it except me.

But time has a way of healing hurts and changing things. As the end of the winter term approached, Mr. Henderson asked my parents to send me to Marion number seven, the school which was rightfully in our district anyway. He explained that the school population there had dropped to only three and that they needed four to keep the school open. So the beginning of the spring term found me, with my lunch bucket, wooden pencil box and second grade reader, moving into a new situation where I was to remain until I finished eighth grade six years later.

That spring term at Marion number seven was almost like being privately tutored when at home the year before, only that in addition to myself I had Wilbert, Rex and his sister Marjorie as school mates.

The following year the population increased and in a year or so we had nearly filled our one-room school. And going to school with its scholastic and social aspects pretty well filled my life a good portion of the year. My world was expanded beyond the boundaries of our farm and near neighbors to include the school district. Before long the extra curricular activities such as school programs at Halloween and Christmas and playing in the school yard (in which our imaginations had full reign, since we had a minimum of playground equipment — a softball and a bat) were something that helped to make me less reluctant to spend so much time at school. We played games such as "anty over" the school house, "pump, pump, pullaway", "red light", "run sheep, run" and other hand-me-down folk games. In the winter there was "fox and goose", snowball fights with snow forts, and just plain frolicking in the snow. When the weather was bad we played inside at such games as "spin the bottle" and chalk games on the blackboard.

After Dean began school I was much happier. The

two of us walked the two miles to and from school together. Our playground was extended to include the road between the farm and the school.

The walk to school was usually a "forced march" to get there before the nine o'clock bell rang. Sometimes when we were late, if one of our friends were on the bell rope, we were able to get into the school house before the bell stopped ringing and thus were not marked "tardy". It got so the neighbors knew when they heard an extended ringing of the school bell in the morning that the Artley boys were running the last few rods to the school house.

Going home after school was a much more leisurely time, however. Sometimes we were even tardy getting home and late getting at our chores. This could be worse than being late to school.

There was much to explore and examine along the rutted, often muddy, country roads. There were bridges to tip-toe over, "just in case a tramp was asleep under it". Roadside trees and shrubs were hosts to small wild creatures that we could sometimes spot if we were quiet. In season there were wildflowers, grape and plum blossoms along the fence rows that filled the air with their scent — adding to that of clover blossoms in the fields nearby. In September there were sweet wild plums with

which we filled our lunch pails and fed upon along the way.

There was a period of time when Rodemeyer's dog intimidated me as I passed by their place. One time during my first year when I walked the road alone, Mrs. Rodemeyer had to rescue me from behind a roadside tree and accompany me safely past their driveway, assuring me that their dog, which seemed friendly enough then, was all bark. Nevertheless for some time after that I took another route home.

More frightening than any dog was an experience I had another time when I was going home alone by the alternate route which included a mile of graveled Iowa Highway number ten. A car pulled up and stopped and the lone man driver asked if I would like a ride. My parents had warned me to never accept rides from strangers, so I declined. He insisted and even started to get out of the car, whereupon I started running down the road toward Ed Mahncke's place hoping our good neighbor would see my plight. But about then the man who was so insistent upon giving me a ride apparently decided I wasn't worth his bother and took off in a cloud of dust.

That experience made me even more cautious of strangers. A few weeks following that episode

another car pulled up beside me on the same stretch of highway. With my heart in my throat I refused the offer of a ride from the middle-aged couple, even though they said they were going right past my driveway. Sometime later the pastor of the Lutheran church about two miles from our place, the vesper bell of which often could be heard on the evening air, told Dad about how he and his wife had tried to give me a ride. He thought my parents had me pretty well trained.

Most of the time our schoolyard gang was an amiable group, but occasionally there were fights. Too often I was one of the protagonists and Roy Spangenburg the other. I have no idea what we fought about — I'm not even sure we knew then.

The last few years I attended country school, Dad served as director of our school. It was with a great sense of pride that I walked into our schoolroom, still reeking from the smell of cigar smoke from the meeting of the night before, knowing that Dad was now director of our school.

It was up to the director to hire the teacher, provide the coal and other supplies, and mow the tall grass in the schoolyard each fall before school opened. During Dad's term of office a fence was put up around the schoolyard and a well was drilled and a pump installed on the school grounds so that we no longer had to go across the road to Mahncke's for drinking water.

But being of the family of the director had its drawbacks as well as its glory. We became aware of this when Dad rehired a teacher that some in the district had expressed dissatisfaction with. This action of Dad's brought about a breach of relations between our family and several of our neighbors. For several months we were made to feel as outcasts in the neighborhood, and we couldn't even go to town without being aware of having fallen from the grace of our neighbors. When we met on the streets, they looked the other way. It was some time before this unpleasant situation healed, even though the scars remained.

On the whole my years at Marion school number seven were happy years, rich in things rural and human. The only adverse result of my years at country school was being made to feel inferior when I entered high school in town. Those of us from the country schools were breaking into a class that had been together since kindergarten in town. We were outsiders and rightly or wrongly, we felt we were being looked down upon.

But if I had to do it all over again, I would choose to spend those early, formative years in a one-room country school, just the way I did back then.

Fun

When I was growing up, "fun" was where we found it — and it could be found about anywhere on the farm. There was very little organized recreation in those days, at least in our part of the world. We played some games that had hand-me-down rules, but most of what we did in the realm of fun we cooked up ourselves.

Our elders sometimes suggested things for us to do — primed the pump, so to speak — and we'd carry on from there. But mostly, when it came to fun, our elders suggested things that we must **not** do.

Being relatively isolated from other children near our age, brother Dean and I were pretty much loners. Our play was mostly around the farmstead where we explored and became familiar with all the interesting places of the house, barn and other buildings and the grove of trees that bordered the buildings on the west and north. We had favorite trees to climb and make "homes" in. The great but-

ternut tree was a favorite play place. We swung and bounced up and down by the hour on its spreading branches that nearly touched the ground. Beneath those branches, we gathered sticky butternuts and raked paths in the soft, leaf-mulched loam to create roads or rooms for play houses.

It was in one of these raked play houses that I first encountered vandalism. Mom had made some crude furniture of chunks of stove wood and boards for our playhouse. One afternoon a neighbor boy, several years older than I, came to our place and before the horrified eyes of Dean and me he proceeded to kick and break up the play furniture. Our cries of protest only seemed to heighten his pleasure. Needless to say he   didn't become one of our playmates and we felt no sorrow when he and the rest of his strange family moved out of the neighborhood.

About half a mile down the road, across the bridge and up the hill, lived one of our earliest playmates.

Kenneth was about four years older than I and an

only child. He and Dean and I spent many pleasant hours together on summer afternoons at his place and at ours.

Kenneth was very handy at making things and made almost all of his own toys using a few simple tools and scraps of lumber, metal and wheels he'd found about the farm. We spent hours at his place playing with the homemade train or threshing machine and steamer or with his Shetland pony, Cleo, and the two-wheeled cart his father made. About four o'clock his mother served us a lunch which often consisted of sandwiches of home-dried beef on homemade buns, chocolate cake and lemonade. When five o'clock came playtime stopped and it was time to go home and start chores.

Other neighborhood playmates were Becky and her little brother MacBurnie. Their parents and our parents became close friends and we kids became as close as cousins. Becky, about Dean's age, was a quiet, shy girl who nevertheless seemed to enjoy the rough and tumble imaginary world of pirates and cowboys and Indians that Dean and I forced upon her. She also shared in our play grocery store that we operated in the granary until we were forced out of business at threshing time when the space was needed for the oat crop.

Mom opened cans and boxes upside down so, that

when empty and arranged on our shelves, they gave a look of realism to our store. Our bananas were corn cobs stuck onto a wire seed corn drying rack, thus resembling a large bunch of bananas as they used to be displayed in the real grocery store. Corn cobs, broken into shorter pieces and wrapped in empty candy bar wrappers, became Baby Ruth and Milky Way bars on our candy shelf. (Thus wrapped, a corn cob looked quite convincing as a candy bar — so much so that one April first Mom successfully pulled an April Fool's joke on Dean and me by placing ''Baby Ruth'' wrapped cobs in our school lunch.)

The prize possession in our store was an old coffee grinder we had found in perfect condition in a dump. It sat on our counter and was a conversation piece to adults who happened in.

When storekeeping got too tame we ventured into piracy or some other adventuresome activity. Becky gamely joined in and even added a learned flavor to our play as she was more acquainted with the world of books than we were.

One summer afternoon Becky, Dean and I set out on a pirate mission to the creek to bury some treasure. Our safari needed a bearer to help carry the shovels, treasure chest and other accouterment of our expedition; we drafted MacBurnie.

76

The trail took us down the cow lane, through the wire and pole pasture gate, along the row of willow, chokecherry and cottonwood trees at the edge of the slough, across the "bogs" to the creek and along that meandering stream until we came to a gravelly place where the cows crossed. Here we prepared to wade across.

We no longer had our bearer, MacBurnie, as he had been left behind under the cottonwoods at the edge of the slough. He wasn't very happy at this. But we reasoned that his was a much better fate than most "pirates" would have allowed to ensure the secrecy of their buried treasure. So we could not fully appreciate the fact that he seemed quite upset at being left behind — even though we had left him with some cookies and a jar of water.

At the creek Becky, Dean and I waded across to a low, grassy mound on the far bank. With our shovels we cut out a square of sod. Then we dug into the sandy loam, sprinkled with tiny bits of snail shells, fossils from an ancient lake bed, and made a hole about twelve inches by twelve inches. We deposited our treasure — some glass beads, and some white and clear quartz pebbles in a wooden cigar box. We replaced the dirt and square of sod, being careful not to leave any evidence of our digging there. Then I took a folded piece of paper from my pocket and with the stub of a pencil drew a map showing the location of our buried treasure. After swearing to secrecy and promising that "years from now" we would return and dig up what we had buried, we went back by the way we had come and rejoined MacBurnie, who by then was in a very foul mood.

That treasure was buried about fifty years ago. Becky is now a librarian at a distant state university. MacBurnie is an instructor of English literature at a college. Dean farms the land on which the treasure is buried and the map is in a place of safe keeping in the old house on the same farm. We may still have the rendezvous on that creek bank. But when we do, I feel it must include our bearer, since he has grown to be a much larger man than me. I would hate the prospect of spending the rest of my days casting uneasy glances over my shoulder. Also, this treasure hunting party should include spouses, children and grandchildren. It would indeed be quite a crowd on that creek bank to witness the excavation of those glass beads and pretty stones.

There were many pleasant hours spent in that creek pasture. In fact the whole farm was our playground, from the creek banks through the groves to the grassy hills of the northeast portion. On those hills we could romp with the clouds and

JUST THINK — NO SCHOOL

I'LL BEAT YA TO THE CREEK

THE FIRST DAY OF SUMMER VACATION — THE CLOSEST I EVER CAME TO FEELING REALLY *FREE*!

BOY, THAT COOL GRASS FEELS GO...OUCH — A THISTLE!

BOB ARTLEY

5-30-78 WORTHINGTON DAILY GLOBE

compete with the bees for the nectar in the clover heads. We also watched the swallows skim over the heads of ripening grain as they darted this way and that gathering flying insects.

It was in those grain fields — nearly ripe oats — that we more than once got into trouble in our pursuit of fun. We found that when walking through the standing grain, it was easy to make a path. The broken-over hollow stalks stayed pressed down. Along with our cousin Harold, who was a year younger than I, Dean and I further discovered that if we crawled on our hands and knees we made broader paths.

One July morning, shortly before the oats was ready to harvest, the three of us spent an hour or two crawling uphill and down, turning this way and that, making beautiful trails through the oats. We not only had "roads" winding through the grain but here and there the "roads" widened into "towns." A large pressed down place we called "Sioux City."

When we were tired of building roads and towns, we made our way back to the farmyard where we were promptly attracted to the kitchen by the pleasant smell of frying doughnuts. As we each consumed one of the fresh pastries we related the fun we'd been having to Mom. Whereupon she sternly suggested we go and tell Dad all about it.

Mom's suggestion completely changed the mood of that sunny summer morning. Suddenly I remembered having been punished before for the same destructive caper. How could I have forgotten?

Being that I was the oldest of the three culprits, and therefore the "responsible" one, it was understood I was the one to make the confession.

Dad was in the shade of a tree in the yard busily repairing the canvas to the oatbinder. I was not anxious to interrupt him at his work, especially since he didn't seem to be in a good mood anyway, due to the poor condition of the worn canvases. I was reluctant to further spoil his day (and mine) by the bit of bad news I had for him. But Dad, discerning by my manner I had something unpleasant to tell him, soon had a confession out of me and pronounced sentence — the worst of which was the lecture on a spoiled oats harvest that accompanied it.

Cousin Harold also shared in other forbidden adventures from time to time, until our elders dreaded the times we got together.

Another such misadventure, caused by a fateful lapse of memory again involving oats harvest, occurred when we were having a hilarious time bouncing on top of a new straw stack. Each step we took on top of the stack made a depression in the

Memories Of A Former Kid.

IT STEERS TOO EASY

WOW— THAT'S DANGEROUS

STOP STOP STOP

WHUMP

THE NEW SLED

12-29-75

BOB ARTLEY
WORTHINGTON DAILY GLOBE

bright, new straw which had been so carefully rounded to shed the rain. This fun was cut short when we spotted Dad approaching with purposeful step while at the same time stripping the leaves from a willow switch he carried. Harold and I made a quick escape down the ladder and into the cornfield. But Dean, in his haste, slipped and fell, unhurt but frightened, into a soft pile of chaff and straw at the base of the stack. He was caught and dealt with immediately. Harold and I, not being able to hide in the corn forever, eventually got what was coming to us, too.

Another time we took the loose end of a ball of twine in the corn binder which was parked at the edge of the grove, and walked up the hill, around the corncrib, across the farmyard and down the lane to the mailbox. Here we came to an abrupt stop, for it was here that Dad caught up with us. He had happened by the binder a few moments before — in time to notice the unwinding spool of twine in its holder. Grabbing and stopping the twine, he followed it to the culprits at the other end.

Barns were always a source of much interest and fun while we were growing up. Our own barn was, of course, home to us. We came to know intimately every cobwebby nook and crevice inside and out. We even made a thrilling ascent to the peak of the roof

one time, climbing by pulling ourselves up the lightning rod cable. As we sat astraddle the ridge pole on the roof we could see over the whole farm. The farmyard and its inhabitants of chickens, cows and pigs looked strange when viewed from our "mountain top." The lightning rods with their blue glass balls and the weather vane pitted and worn by the elements had always seemed as something akin to the stars. Now we had brought them down to earth.

Other barns with which we became familiar to a lesser degree were those on Grandpa's and my uncle's farms. Grandpa's was a broad sprawling barn like ours, only the hay mow came all the way to the ground in the center. Pigeons strutted and cooed in the rafters and made a noisy exit amid a flapping of wings when we entered the barn. Uncle George's barn was enormous, with cavernous mows in which we would climb and jump into great piles of hay.

Uncle Walter also had a large barn. It was much older in years as well as in style than any of the others we knew, being a basement barn on the side of a hill. The upper portion, accessible by two huge doors that rolled on tracks, was where many tons of hay and grain could be stored, as well as wagons and other farm implements. Two tall louvered vents were in each end of this fine old barn and provided

air for the great mounds of curing hay piled within. The large beams that spanned this mow were excellent for walking along and jumping from into the piles of hay. Within the limestone walls of the lower or basement portion of the barn were kept the horses, calves and milk cows.

Uncle Wayne's barn was small, almost toy-like, as was his farm. It was cozy and no less fun to play in. Uncle Dallas had a barn of modern design made of brick and mortar. It was furnished with the latest in automatic milking equipment. We didn't play here much but instead watched in awe as the great Brown Swiss cows were milked by machine.

Much of our fun was in the form of family gatherings on various holidays, birthdays and in-between. Christmas and the Fourth of July, at opposite ends of the seasons, provided occasions for family get-togethers. Christmas was an all-time favorite because of the presents involved, but the Fourth of July was a close second.

Sometimes the clan gathered at Maine's grove south of Hampton. This was an undeveloped, semi-public place with a broad creek and tall elm, hickory and oak trees. We could almost count on one of the kids getting soaked by accidently sitting down while wading in the creek.

At other times we gathered at Klousia's timber where Uncle George made a special effort to provide for our comfort by shutting the cows in another pasture and setting up makeshift picnic tables of planks and barrels.

At these summer gatherings, fried chicken, roasting ears, homemade ice cream and watermelon were part of the fare. Some of the images that parade through my mind of those distant summers are: adults sitting on running boards of the cars or stretched out on blankets visiting about crops, politics and family; kids playing, fighting and eating watermelon, spitting the seeds and standing with legs spread apart to keep the juice from adding to the grass stains on trousers and skirts; softball games; mothers fanning flies from sleeping babies; and Grandpa, smoking his pipe and viewing the whole scene with the silent wisdom of his accumulated years.

Firecrackers sometimes were smuggled in at the Fourth of July family gatherings. But the adults, for obvious reasons, forbid this form of celebration until each family was at home. We looked forward to the treat with great anticipation.

Fireworks were legal at the time and newspapers were filled with accounts of fingers being blown off, eyes put out and tragic fires caused by careless use of fireworks. These stories brought stern warnings

80

A CHEAP, SAFE WAY TO CELEBRATE THE FOURTH OF JULY WAS TO TURN THE IGNITION SWITCH OFF AND ON AS WE DROVE ALONG.

BANG
POP
BANG
BANG POP

BOB ARTLEY
7-3-78 WORTHINGTON DAILY GLOBE

and sobering thoughts concerning the use of these dangerous toys. But they didn't dampen our enthusiasm or anticipation of the great holiday. For days and weeks before the Fourth, we would visit the fireworks displays in the different stores in town and try to balance our longings for the rockets, silver fountain cones, cherry bombs, spit devils, Roman candles, sparklers, pin wheels, the giant four-inchers and roll caps for our cap guns to the few coins in our pockets. We were all too concious of how quickly a dollar could be "blown" leaving only the pungent smell of powder, burnt-out remains and the memory of the "bang."

On the night of the Fourth, after it was "dark enough" our family gathered on our back steps. First we lit the sparklers. They competed with the fire flies that flickered off and on over the lawn against the dark shadows of the grove. Then there were the Roman candles. Each of us kids took turns shooting them to make our display last as long as possible. One time Dad bought a sky rocket for us. This was quite a treat as they were expensive. He made a slanted trough to launch it from. It was a great moment when he touched the smoldering punk to its fuse and stepped back as first it hissed and then took off in a great "swoosh" over the trees and exploded into a beautiful shower of colored sparks

high over the corn field north of the grove. We kids spent a good part of the next morning looking among the green corn for the spot where the burned-out shell had fallen to earth.

One Fourth of July night, after we'd had our own family fireworks display, we noticed a red glow on the horizon behind the barn. We knew it must be a fire, so all climbed into the Model "T" and headed down the road to see where it was.

It was a farm house three miles east of our place. Cars and people lined the road and watched as flames consumed the house while friends and neighbors made futile attempts to douse the fire with water from a well pumped dry.

It was said the fire had been started by fireworks. Whether this was true or not, it caused us to hurry home and once again check to be sure there were no smoldering remains of a Roman candle or sparkler.

By far the greatest part of our outdoor fun was during the warm months of the year when the whole universe seemed inviting. Even in the summer the daylight hours seemed too short and we played into the twilight and dusk before being dragged off to baths and bed. But when permitted, playing in the dusk had its own special fun. Usually play then was of scary things such as bears and other wild animals or spooks.

Every summer we looked forward to Uncle Will's visit from Sioux City. When he and his family arrived we kids knew we were in for some of our scariest fun. Cousin Verl, about four years older than I, was a storehouse of ghost stories. Every summer she came supplied with a fresh batch of "Fu Manchu" movies she had seen the previous year. She told these stories to us after dark with appropriate voice and sound effects as we sat in the back seat of their family's Overland touring car with side curtains. By the time she finished our eyes were as big as saucers and every hair on our heads stood at attention. Every shadow and sound in the darkened farmyard seemed related to her tale until finally we all, including Verl, made a dash for the house and the grown-ups.

As we grew older there came a time when Verl became bored with the company of her immature boy cousins and it was next to impossible to get her to join in our play. Thus it was that we should have suspected something when she voluntarily joined us on a particular occasion.

We were spending the day at Aunt Bertha's farm. At the noon meal there was talk of a "crazy" man who had escaped the authorities and had been seen in the neighborhood. This bit of news did not escape the notice of Harold, Dean and I who were prone to wander about the farm on exploring expeditions without permission — one such expedition having been that very morning. So in view of this bit of news we were again warned not to leave the farmyard. As the afternoon wore on, however, concern over the warning diminished as our play took us farther and farther from the house yard. At last we were as far as we could go and still obey the warning. We were climbing in a row of ash trees in a cow lane that was bordered on the one side by the barnyard and on the other by a field of green corn in full tassel. Each of us sat in a separate tree.

We were pleasantly surprised at the sudden arrival of Verl and promptly invited her to climb one of the vacant trees and join in the fun. But before she could adequately reply to our invitation, there was a great commotion at the edge of the corn field next to the lane fence. From between the rows of corn emerged a bent figure in tattered coat and a battered old hat pulled down over a scowling, bearded face. He was emitting inhuman growls and seemed to be foaming at the mouth, while threshing the corn stalks with a stick.

First a moment of stunned silence, then in unison from the trees came the terrified cry, "crazy man!" Three pairs of legs dropped from the leafy branches, and were already full speed ahead when they touched the ground. Since the object of our terror threatened to cut off our retreat to the house,

we first hurriedly negotiated a hog tight barbed wire fence, sailed over two board gates and finally arrived at the house yard. Here, to our dismay, we found Grandpa doubled up in laughter, apparently unconcerned about the threat to his progeny. At about the same time we remembered we'd left Verl to face the creature alone, only to discover she was bringing up the rear in a most casual manner and wearing a peculiar expression (not one of fear) on her face.

There followed a series of revelations: Uncle Will, with corn silk on his face and in a borrowed tattered barn jacket and hat, was part of a conspiracy to keep us from wandering afar; Harold discovered a rather severe cut on his toe which he hadn't been aware of before; Dean had lost all his color and seemed to be somewhat in a state of shock which in turn caused Mom and the rest of the adults concern and remorse; I had come through the experience visibly unscathed but vaguely in question of the method used to teach us a lesson — and also feeling more than ever the generation gap that separated Verl and us.

This experience (which we have all had many laughs over since) didn't change the fact that we kids continued to look forward to the annual summer visit of Uncle Will and his family.

We spent many hours making things; toy airplanes, boats, farm buildings and forts. Some of them were crude, but where the things we made lacked realism, we filled in with our imaginations.

My first year in high school I met John Lambert, a lanky, red-haired classmate whose manual training bench was next to mine. We soon discovered we had similar interests in boats and from this introduction developed a friendship.

When John and I were in our senior year, we and Dean started construction of a boat. It was of our own design, sixteen feet long and four feet "abeam". The sides were twelve inches deep and when launched, it "drew" about two inches of water. The front end tapered in slightly and was covered by a deck. We also had a poop deck and two boards for seats amidships. What it lacked in grace of line was made up for in sturdiness.

We started it in our empty corn crib. The construction of it, like ocean-going vessels many times its size, took months. We had full schedules of work and school and it was hard to find free time. When fall came and the crib was needed to store the corn harvest, we discovered that our enthusiasm had blinded us to an important structural fact — we couldn't get the unfinished boat through the door. Dad wouldn't let us tear open the end of the crib, so our only alternative was to dismantle what we had so laboriously constructed.

This embarassing situation proved to be a blessing, however, since we were able to redesign and construct a much better craft the second time. This we accomplished in an empty portion of the hay mow. When finished we used the hay fork ropes to hoist it and lower the finished craft onto sawhorses in the farmyard where it was painted white and grey with its name "Anonymous" neatly lettered in black. We selected that name after we couldn't agree on any other.

We had many plans for the use of Anonymous involving different waters, including a trip down the Mississippi river. But our noble craft's active life was destined to be short. We launched and enjoyed it on Beed's Lake, three miles from our home, for one season. Before we were able to take it out of the lake and store it for the winter it fell victim to the famous Armistice Day blizzard of 1940. Our boat was swamped where it was tied to its wharf and was frozen in where it remained all winter. When the ice broke up in the spring we were able to empty it of mud and water and take it home to clean and repaint. But the life seemed to have gone out of it. A rot set in and before long the Anonymous was no longer seaworthy. It became a decaying hulk in our grove — a symbol of some boyish dreams that also were decaying.

Saturday night, especially in the summer, was a special time in our social life. We usually tried to come in from the fields earlier than usual and get the chores and milking done. After a hurried supper we bathed and dressed for town and then all piled into the Ford, kids in the back seat, being careful of the egg crate with its fragile contents, and headed for town.

It wasn't dark yet when we arrived but already the parking places were taken, so we drove round and round after dropping off the crate of eggs at the grocery where we traded until we found a place to squeeze the car into. The prime parking places were on main street in front of the stores where the crowds were walking back and forth. But these places were taken by the first into town, and it was even said that some of the townspeople parked their cars there in the afternoon and then walked downtown in the evening to sit in them and watch people. After the car was parked and the time was set to reassemble for the trip home, Dad, Mom and our little brother Dan, went off to shop and visit with friends and acquaintances they met on the streets. Dean and I took off to meet cousin Harold at a prearranged spot. Then with a few cents burning in our pockets, we set off for the Sweet Shop to get our usual stick licorice at a penny a stick.

Stocked with several sticks of the candy, we crossed the street to the courthouse square where we climbed the stone steps of the courthouse and ate licorice, talked and "spit brown". After the licorice was gone we played tag up and down the steps and in and around the shrubbery of the courthouse grounds until we tired of that. Then we joined the "Saturday night parade" around the square until the big four-faced clock at the top of the courthouse "bonged" ten times which was our signal to head for the car.

After the "goodbyes" were said and our family once again was loaded into the car, with the egg crate this time filled with groceries, we drove up to the little popcorn stand on the corner and Dad bought us each a five cent bag of popcorn to munch on our way home.

It was only a few miles home but quite often we were asleep in the back seat when Dad announced that we were home and we sleepily stumbled into the house and into bed.

After we boys had outgrown the courthouse rendezvous and the licorice, we slicked down our hair a little more carefully than usual and walked through the crowds on the sidewalks hoping we might encounter our current heart interest. If we should by chance, and the particular girl gave a smile of recognition as she and her girl companions passed by, the evening was a success and we were ready to go home to nourish the memory of that sweet encounter in our dreams for the next week as we went about our work in the fields and barnyard.

From an early age I found girls interesting. This may have been due, in part, to the fact they were fairly rare in my experience, since we didn't raise girls on our farm. For even though there was Becky and my girl cousins (I had eight in all) in our young lives, we did not see them on a day to day basis.

My first real date was late in high school when I managed to muster enough courage to ask Janet to go to the Junior-Senior banquet with me. I was so painfully shy that my natural clumsiness was compounded, my feeble attempts at conversation fell flat and I made all kinds of "goofs" — besides spilling my water glass at the banquet table. I'm sure it must have been a miserable evening for my date.

Back in the country school it was Evelyn I was shy and clumsy around. We often asked permission to go together for coal for the stove and water for the water cooler in the vestibule. We also received permission to study our spelling lesson together (we were the only two in our grade) now and then. We secretly held hands as we sat side by side in the old-fashioned double school desks. Those study sessions are sweet to the memory. I only hope Evelyn learned to spell better than I did as a result.

I wasn't very monogamous in my girl interest but could be easily attracted to a new interest on short notice. As a result I had many heart interests when I got into high school where there were so many girls, even though the objects of my secret affections never knew it. My cousin John and I, in the same class in high school, shared a girl at one time — only in our fantasies, however — for she was beautiful and popular and hardly knew we existed.

When I was twelve or thirteen I fell violently in love with a trapeze performer at the Franklin County fair. No one knew of my "affair" — certainly not the girl who must have been three or four years my senior. But I missed a lot of the other features of the fair that year as I watched every afternoon and every evening performance she gave. At the front of the standing crowd with my elbows on the stage in front of the grandstand I feasted my eyes on this attractive girl clad in tights that accentuated her comely, shapely body as she performed with grace and beauty as I had never seen before.

My heart was heavy as I watched her last performance on the last night of the fair. The bright lights of the open air stage seemed as unaware of the full harvest moon over the fairgrounds as that lovely girl was of me in that sea of faces looking up at her as she made her graceful bow at the finale of the act.

My family wondered at my pensive mood as we drove homeward that night. They seemed to think I was sad because our 4-H calf had been sold at auction that day. I was content to leave it at that.

The Creek

The stream that flowed through our farm probably did more to establish the character of the place than any other feature. It entered on the west border just after flowing under the wooden bridge on the township road, meandered through about twenty acres of slough land, cut out through our south border where it ran for about fifty yards or so in our neighbor's land before returning to our farm under the line fence. Here it splashed over some stones, curved around a willow-lined bank and wandered through another twenty acres of slough before exiting into our neighbor's land to the east of us.

The creek and its surrounding marshland affected about seventy-five to eighty acres of the farm. Dad resented it for the practical reason that it took tillable land from the farm. In his later years he was able to drain part of the slough, adding more plow ground to the farm.

However, when we were growing up, the creek

area of the farm was a wonderful place to be. My brothers and I spent many hours there throughout many years. And it's only fair to say that Dad, as well as the rest of the family, found a special sort of pleasure in this somewhat primeval place.

The creek land served as our permanent pasture. It was low ground and remained green and lush late into the summer when high pastureland was dry and sparse.

We usually turned the cows to pasture in late April or early May, depending on how tall the grass was and how well the winter feed supply held out. Before we could take the cattle to the pasture for the season we had to inspect and repair the fences. The winter storms often blew down tree branches or whole trees, ruining sections of fence. Or the frost over the winter would heave a post, leaving it high and weakened in the fence line. But we knew for certain the creek fence would have to be repaired or completely rebuilt because of the spring floods and ice flows.

It was enjoyable to inspect the fence line in the spring. There was the smell of greening vegetation, the clean, fresh appearance of familiar haunts not seen without snow cover since the previous fall. We heard the excited twitter and songs of the birds returned from their winter refuge and busily establishing their territories and their nesting. The song of the meadowlark and the "cherree" of the redwing blackbird particularly stand out as the background music to fixing up the creek fence.

Aside from the setting and the spring atmosphere surrounding us, fixing fence was not a pleasant task. We grumbled about it plenty. The force of the flood waters usually wiped out not only the portion of the fence spanning the creek, but several yards on either side because of the width of the flood stream. It was understood that we wouldn't put new wire across the creek if the old rusted wire could be salvaged. This was a formidable task, searching through mud-encrusted trash and tree limbs for the twisted, broken strands of barbed wire. Despite our leather gloves, it also meant scratches, snags and even punctures to our hands, arms or elsewhere when we were caught in a writhing, twisting strand of that rusty wire we were trying to tame. Those wounds meant the additional sting of being daubed with mercurochrome or iodine when returning home.

We wore knee-high rubber boots when fixing creek fence and usually found ourselves sitting on the bank pouring water out of a boot we'd mistakenly thought taller than the water was deep. But I enjoyed the feel of the force of the stream against my booted legs and the challenge of trying to stand up against that force. The creek has been known to win in that struggle, leaving a very wet challenger the butt of hearty laughter from those remaining dry.

The creek, Spring Creek by name, was a spring fed creek. Even during some quite extensive droughts in the 1930's, there was always at least a trickle of water running through our pasture. The springs also meant the creek was never completely frozen over in the winter and was unsafe for skating. However, we did explore its frozen course in winter as well as summer and more than once hurried homeward on a cold winter day with ice-encrusted boots and pants and with ice water squishing around our toes.

But the seasons of spring, summer and autumn blended together as a time when the creek and its domain was our land of enchantment. For several years after we were old enough to venture from the farmyard, the creek was a playground without equal. It had everything a child needed to nurture a lively imagination and an interest in the world of nature.

As the creek meandered through the slough land of our farm the channel followed an ancient lake of which the shoreline is still discernable. My grandfather Artley (who died when my Dad was three-years-old) planted cottonwood and willow trees along a portion of the north shoreline, thereby forming a line of demarcation between slough and plowland. He also planted some ash trees along one side of what he must have intended to be a building site. He built a house there which served as his home for awhile before he married my grandmother. Later his house was moved to the present farmyard site and used as a granary.

There were other trees that came up naturally on a slight rise of ground on the northeastern edge of the ancient lake. These were mostly boxelder, with some wild cherry and a couple of black walnut trees.

A second, smaller stream drained a watershed area mostly encompassing our farm and part of our neighbors to the north and northeast into Spring Creek. Along it were many gnarled old willows, a few boxelders, cottonwood trees, and one sturdy old black walnut tree that shaded a large grey boulder. The site of this tree and boulder was established as a picnic place — the flat side of the boulder being a place to build a fire.

Once when I was quite small Mom brought Dean and me and a picnic lunch to this spot. This small stream, besides being a channel for the watershed had some springs that fed it. My grandfather used one of those springs as a place to keep wild strawberries in glass jars. The cold of the spring water kept them as fresh as when he picked them from a nearby grassy bank.

That spring — at least in its original condition — was gone when we were small but there were still springs in the stream bed where one could see clean sand boiling up. Those places were fun to step into when wading. The water was cold and the bubbling sand tickled the feet.

Mom, Dean, and I took off our shoes and stockings after our picnic lunch and went wading. Mom was wading ahead of us in the small, shallow stream when she stepped into one of the bubbly sand patches and started to sink. She sank nearly to her knees before she was able to back out. That brought an end to our wading that day and a warning never to go near that spot again. In the years that followed we were cautious about where we stepped when we roamed along the creek.

There was a similar hazard in the form of a large sinkhole in an adjoining pasture farther down the stream. As we approached the large, slime-covered mud hole, the sod beneath our step shook and trembled much as if it were underlaid with gelatin. Calves were known to wander into that sinkhole and disappear from sight. Even a horse is said to have been lost in its mucky depths.

There was still another sinkhole, or in this case, quicksand bed, that nearly changed the course of history (for Artleys at least). It was about a mile downstream from our farm in a marshy place where willow thickets grew in profusion. A little girl of about ten or twelve — who years later told this story to her small grandson as he listened in wide-eyed wonder — went to fetch the milk cows from the creek pasture. As she crossed through an unfamiliar part of the pasture to head off an errant cow she suddenly stepped into a morass and found herself being sucked downward. Quickly she grabbed some overhanging branches of the willow thicket and was able to pull herself to safety. Her father, my great-grandfather, returned to the spot with a twenty-foot pole and could not touch bottom.

As Grandma Artley told me of this I was thankful she had been spared, and I pondered the workings of fate that later gave her a son who was my father who caused me to be living and enjoying the very creek and its sloughs that nearly wiped out our branch of the family.

Most of the creek was shallow so one could wade across easily. Where the current moved quite swiftly over pebbles or stones, splashing and making a happy watery sound, sometimes I saw crayfish darting backwards, "chubs" and minnows or perhaps a carp streaking through the waving water weeds. But there were pools here and there that

were deep and quiet where the dragonflys flitted back and forth on a lazy summer day and the water bugs scooted in senseless circles, apparently in some kind of water carnival. Adding to the carnival atmosphere were the water walkers, those insects on high stilt-like legs that utilized the natural surface tension of the water with their long, pontoon-like feet.

When I was small and time seemed to be as plentiful as the sun-warmed air around me, I sometimes just laid on the grassy bank, taking it all in, nourishing my spirit. There were times when I felt as though I needed nothing else in life and would be content to spend my entire life in the creek pasture observing and becoming familiar with every natural aspect of that fascinating world, drawing and painting the myriad forms of life that were in that ancient lake bottom. I still feel that would have been a rewarding and worthwhile life.

Our favorite pool site was where the creek made an easy bend against a fairly high grassy bank in the shade of the ancient willows. Nearby was a lone, tall cottonwood which had waxy leaves that rattled in the breeze. We sometimes picnicked on this bank or sat with a willow or bamboo pole and a line dangling into the water and a can of worms or dough balls beside us on the grass. When the homemade cork bobber began sending out concentric rings on the surface of the quiet pool we tensed and waited for it to be pulled under. Perhaps we had hooked a three or four inch "chub," or perhaps a bullhead, or — with great excitement — an eight or ten inch carp. Quite often we threw them back so they could grow larger and provide us with more sport another time. Or we carried them home in a pail of water and dumped them in the stock tank where they sometimes lived for years on the moss and spilled grain.

But sometimes our pitiful catch was taken home and Mom fried it, providing us with two or three bites — at least a taste of fish.

On one of our creek bank fishing expeditions, Dad caught a carp that must have been a long-time resident of those parts. He measured about fifteen inches long. The old carp must have been as surprised as we were when Dad pulled him from the water. There was quite a tussle in the grass on that creek bank as Dad worked the hook out of the carp's mouth and put that large (by our standards) flopping fish into the pail of water. Dad figured the old fellow must have been yawning from boredom and accidently ran into the hook with his mouth open.

We put that carp in the stock tank with the other fish where he lived for several months until one cold morning the tank ran over and he lay cold and lifeless next to the wooden stock tank. Mom cooked him and he was delicious — apparently living those months in the fresh water in the stock tank had removed the characteristic mud taste that carp have.

The pools of our creek also were our "swimming holes." They weren't deep enough to do any real swimming, but we spent many hours paddling and splashing around with as much if not more enjoyment than in a fancy chlorinated pool. In some places the bottom was soft mud and in others, pebbles or sand with cold water coming up through it — one of the many springs. When we'd finished our "swims" we had to inspect our bodies for blood suckers or leeches that sometimes attached themselves between our toes or elsewhere and had to be removed. The most natural and immediate reaction was to grab the slimy, muscular little blob of a creature and pull it loose. It would stretch like a rubber band before letting loose. But if it had been attached a long time it would be gorged with blood (our blood) and was harder to remove.

Sometimes Dean and I went skinny dipping when we went after the cows at chore time, if we were far enough from the road so as not to be seen by passersby. And when cultivating corn on a hot day — if the field weren't too far from the creek — we let the horses rest and took a dip. We didn't worry about not having a towel to dry ourselves. Since it was so hot we soon were dry after putting our clothes on.

Another body of water on our farm was also important to us. This was a small pond in our pasture that was completely cut off from the creek but was only a few feet from it. The pool itself might have been twenty feet in diameter. Surrounding the pool grew rushes and cattails in a marshy ring of mud and water. During most of the summer months the pool itself was covered with lily pads on which frogs sat and among which turtles popped up the tips of their noses to sample the air. In season there were waxy lily flowers whose freshness — we learned — would not survive a trip to the house to adorn the supper table.

We kids called this the Mystic Pool. It seemed most in its element when enveloped in dense fog. When we approached a red wing blackbird perched on one of the swaying willow whips from a half-dead stump screeched its concern for our nearness to its nest somewhere in the rushes.

I've had a lifelong, abiding interest in boats of all kinds. Thus, I suppose, it was only natural to imagine this rather small creek to be a large, navigable river. Dean and I made many small craft in our farm workshop, working mostly with hand saws, draw knife, plane, brace and bit, tin shears, hammer and nails. Our materials consisted of scraps of lumber of all descriptions, preferably light, soft spruce that came from storm-felled trees in our farmyard. We also used pieces of galvanized sheet metal from a discarded hog waterer, string and some pieces of worn out bed sheets from which Mom made us sails.

Because the creek twisted and turned every which way, we could not use sails to propel our small fleet (the sails were only for effect) and since we had no way of providing motor power, we used tow lines — one end attached to the boat and the other to a willow stick like a fish pole. Then we walked along the banks towing our small craft loaded with freight or imaginary passengers or even pirates.

Some of the worst naval battles that ever occurred took place on Spring Creek. Many a ship was lost in battle after being bombarded from the creek bank with clods of dirt or small stones.

One summer a special ship was built (with not too much care) and loaded with flammable material, some large firecrackers, and a candle. After carefully arranging the incendiary sequence we lit the candle and pushed the doomed craft into a quiet pool of the creek. Presently smoke billowed from amidships, then a flame leaped into the rigging. Within moments the small craft was all aflame, and we were dancing with excitement on the creekbank, anticipating the final explosion that would send the gallant craft to the bottom of the channel amid smoke and flame. The pop of one of the firecrackers put out the fire and scattered scorched debris and the rest of the unexploded firecrackers onto the surface of the water. It wasn't as we'd planned, but our imaginations filled in the gaps.

With hammer, saw and more scrap boards we built wharves or piers at different locations up and down the creek. Then with our boats we carried our cargos from port to port. One of those ports was at the base of a high bank that had a vein of grey clay running through it. We dug the clay out of the bank and fashioned small houses, forts and other buildings on the side of this steep bank where the cattle (more dangerous than our pirates) could not trample them. The clay had a rust-like impurity in it that was the basis for our name of the place "Rusty Cove." To this day our family refers to that particular bank and bend in the creek as "Rusty Cove."

One of our most often-carried cargos was peppermint that grew in clumps along the creek bank. We picked the fragrant herb and formed it into bunches that could be carried on our little ships. The smell of a bit of crushed peppermint along a meadow stream still brings back visions of those sunny days along Spring Creek under the willows. And I can hear, in my mind's ear, the song of the redwing blackbird, the croaking of the frogs, and the plaintive cry of the Kildeer.

WHEN THE COAL TRAIN WAS FINALLY BROUGHT IN AND A FUEL CRISIS WAS AVERTED,

BOBARTLEY
1-27-77 WORTHINGTON DAILY GLOBE

Old Fido

I'm not sure where or how it got its name, but the creaky old train that ran on the branch line of the Minneapolis and St. Louis (M.&St.L.) about half or three-quarters of a mile from our place, was known as "Fido" for as far back as I can remember. There was a vague story that it once ran over a dog by that name.

The railroad ran from Hampton northwestward through the towns of Latimer, Alexander, Belmond and finally ended at Kanawha. The steam locomotive and its string of box cars, stock cars, gondola and tank cars followed by its red caboose came wheezing, clanking and swaying westward through our neighborhood every morning about 9 o'clock (you couldn't set your watch by it) and returned toward Hampton somewhere in the vicinity of four o'clock. The two long and two short blasts of its whistle and the plume of smoke from the engine's stack announced its approach. But aside from its melodic whistle it was quiet and did

little to disturb the peaceful countryside it was so much a part of — the only sound being a low rumble and clatter of its flanged wheels on the crooked track, the creaking and groaning of the swaying cars and the soft chuffing of its steam pistons. It never traveled fast — it wasn't safe to do so.

Fido was a friendly presence in our neighborhood and its crew was a part of our population, even though we knew none of them individually or personally (only a waving acquaintance).

Dean and I often walked the railroad on our way to or from school. We'd see who could walk the rails the longest, one foot ahead of the other. Or we stepped from wooden tie to wooden tie, careful not to trip over the uneven way they lay on the roadbed. The end of these railroad hikes usually found our pockets heavy with at least an iron spike or two, some interesting pebbles or a huge nut that had jiggled loose from a railroad car.

The railroad right of way was probably the

longest strip of generally undisturbed prairie around. In season there were many wild flowers to enjoy and sometimes pick to take home to Mom. There were brown-eyed susans, violets, salsify, goldenrod and horsemint among others. Also there were wild plum thickets and pussy willows and cat-tails and other interesting growing things.

We found it especially interesting if the train came by while we were walking along the track. When we first saw the black smoke at a distance or heard Fido's tooooot, tooooot, toot, toot, we would put an ear to the rail until we heard the rumble transmitted through the steel. Careful coaching by our parents and our observation of how those massive wheels flattened nails or washers or an occasional penny sacrificed on the steel rails gave us great respect for the dangers of the train. We got off the track well in advance of the oncoming train and kept at a respectful distance, waving shyly at the engineer and fireman and then the crew in the caboose as it clattered by. Then we ran down the side of the cut to the track to examine the flattened object we had placed on the rail.

One spring our country school had its annual picnic in a pasture on a wooded hillside not far from Fido's tracks. After our picnic meal we kids were exploring the railroad right of way and discovered the section crew had temporarily abandoned a section car flatbed along the track. This gave us an idea and we soon surrounded the small section car, like so many ants around a crust of bread, pushing and lifting and shoving until we had its four wheels in place on the rails. Then our motley crew — boys and girls of all ages and sizes dressed in denims and ginghams — pushed the vehicle about a quarter mile up the gentle slope of the track and climbed aboard. With an initial shove by some of the larger boys we were off on our downhill ride, clickety, clackety at a fun speed until the car finally slowed to a halt on a level stretch of track. Then off we got, and pushed it back up the slope for another ride down. We continued this activity for an hour or so until our teacher, Miss Honeck, thought it might be getting too close to train time. Then we heaved and shoved until we returned the car to where we had found it.

I have no idea what the railroad crew or officialdom would have done had they caught us in this illegal use of their equipment. But we did no damage and left nothing the worse for wear. I suspect the crews would have been tolerant of our game. They occasionally added a little variation to their routine also.

One autumn on the opening of the pheasant-hunting season, Old Fido was moving a little slower

MARCH FIRST WAS MOVING DAY—REGARDLESS OF THE WEATHER. MY BROTHER AND I ENVIED THE KIDS THAT HAD THE ADVENTURE OF EXPLORING A NEW FARM EVERY YEAR OR SO.

BOBARTLEY
3-1-78 WORTHINGTON DAILY GLOBE

than usual as it clattered and clanked and creaked and groaned on its morning trip west. Out of the tall grass between the tracks and the fence bordering the right of way some pheasants exploded into the air and headed on frantic wings toward a field of ripe corn. Two successive shots came from the muzzle of a shotgun protruding from the cab window of the locomotive and one of the pheasants plummeted into the grass just inside the railroad fence. The train rolled on until the caboose was opposite the spot of the fallen bird and then came to a stop. The brakeman swung down from the rear platform, trotted over, picked up the pheasant and climbed back aboard the caboose. A tall column of smoke shot up from the stack of the engine as the train resumed its journey.

There was another railroad, the Chicago Great Western, about a mile south of the M&St.L branch line. This too ran east and west. It was a mainliner that carried passenger trains as well as freight. It was, of course, a much better built and maintained line and the trains were longer and faster than those on "our" railroad. On summer nights, as I lay in an upstairs bedroom drifting off to sleep, the sound of the shrill, lonely whistle of the westbound passenger train turned my thoughts to the mysterious, far away places I read about in books. If I should arouse

myself and go to the south window I could see the lighted windows of the passenger cars streaking through the darkness and I wondered who the people were and where they were going.

During the 1930's it was a fairly common sight to see a hobo or two sitting in the open door of an empty box car. It was against railroad policy for anyone to hitch a ride on a freight. However, those were hard times and the train crews tended to look the other way as these hard luck vagabonds roamed the country looking for a new start. These so-called "bums" were not the professional hobos of the 1920's and earlier.

I can remember some of the real hobos. We kids, when small, were terrified of these "tramps," as we called them. If we saw one of those dark figures (their non-descript clothes were usually dark, partly because of the dirt ground into them) with a pack over his shoulder moving up the road, we ran for the house and peeked out the window to see whether or not they passed our driveway.

I remember a time when a hobo came to our back door and Mom gave him a sandwich and a cup of coffee. Dean and I stood at some distance, peeking around the corner of the house watching him. Mom had neglected to give him a spoon, so without a word he put a long, dirty index finger into the cup and stirred sugar into the coffee.

Another night at about dusk a hobo came to our back door to ask it he could sleep in our barn. Dad, being afraid of a barn fire, refused his request but suggested a vacant barn down the road.

One morning on our way to school we decided to walk down the railroad. It was a foggy early spring morning. Dean and I each walked a rail, carrying our lunch pails at the end of extended arms as we balanced like some kind of birds with our wings out. We hadn't gone far down the track when suddenly there appeared out of the fog ahead a figure in a long, dark coat. We both saw it and without a word wheeled about as one and scooted back to the crossing and continued the rest of the way by road. We cast several uneasy glances over our shoulders to be sure the distance between us and the ominous figure in the fog was getting greater, and when he beckoned us toward him, we moved even faster away.

It was sometime later that Dad related to us a conversation he'd had with a neighbor, Bill Elphic, who had laughingly told of his encounter with us on the railroad tracks that foggy morning when he was looking for some calves that had strayed.

Not only was Old Fido much a part of our local scene it was important to our lives in a practical way. It served the elevator and lumber and coal yards of Latimer, three miles west of our place, as well as the creamery and stockyards in that town.

One severe winter in the 1930's, snow blocked roads and railroads causing a coal shortage in our area. Dad and Dean and I took the team and bobsled to Latimer to get coal and other supplies. The three miles to Latimer was mostly blocked to travel even by bobsled and we made several detours into fields parallel to the road. When we got to Latimer we found the streets lined with many other horse-drawn bobsleds. The coal train had not arrived.

We waited with several other farmers in the coal yard office warming ourselves around the coal-burning stove. As the men talked of the hard winter and the hard times (this being during the great Depression) they glanced impatiently out the frost-lined window at the empty railroad tracks that stretched eastward and disappeared around a curve.

Excitement was stirred a couple of times when someone thought they saw a glimpse of the hoped-for train. Finally a withered old man with a heavy cap with ear flaps that nearly hid his sunken grey jaws as well as his ears, and who frequented the coalyard, stockyard and lumberyard offices to be where the farmers gathered, suddenly raised from his chair beside the stove and, lifting his cane, pointed out the window and said, "there she com-

es!" All chatter stopped and all heads turned the direction he was pointing.

Sure enough, his old eyes were the first to see a bit of black smoke on the horizon.

It was some time before the slow-moving train, pulling cars loaded with coal and pushing a flat car with a snowplow on its front end, deposited the coal-laden cars on the siding beside the empty coal sheds. Soon we, along with several others, were up on the coal train unloading the long-awaited black energy into the waiting bobsleds pulled alongside.

Many changes took place in our neighborhood over the years. After World War II a diesel engine replaced the steam locomotive on the M&St.L branch and "Fido" was never the same again. Then in a few short years the trains stopped running altogether, and later still work crews came and tore up the tracks and hauled away the steel rails and burned the dilapitated wood cross ties. Then the fences came out and first buldozers, then farm tractors and plows obliterated what was a very important part of our lives.

Not long ago I stopped my car on what once had been the rail crossing on our road. Gone was the white post with the white crossed arms that warned travelers on the road of the "RR Crossing." And gone too was the bumpy crossing — a plank, a steel rail, two more planks, a second rail and one more plank — now the road was smooth. I got out of the car and stood in the spot where the crossing once had been and looked west. There before me was a cornfield stretching away to the horizon. It was a green sea that had completely innundated the railroad that once had been there. The late afternoon sunlight glinted off the leaves rustling in the gentle summer breeze much as it would have off the waves of a real sea.

I glanced at my watch. It was almost four o'clock. In the nostalgic mood I was in I thought I heard the far away two long and two short blasts of a steam whistle. Without trying too hard I thought I saw a plume of black smoke beyond the low hill on the horizon where Fido first appeared from this crossing. I got back into the car and drove on. After all, one wouldn't want to be parked on the crossing when a train was coming.

Dreams

Our farm not only nurtured livestock, crops and all manner of growing things of field and meadow, it also was a place where dreams flourished. My young parents, as they established our farm, seemed to understand that without dreams, life would not be of much value. They had left a promising, secure family situation to strike out on their own, to make a home and build a family on a lonely, rundown farm which had been robbed of its soil's fertility by indifferent or dishonest tenants.

Dad's dreams were mostly of a down-to-earth, practical nature. They had to do with building up the farm to where his family might know security in its growing years and to the point where it would be a thriving legacy for whomever chose to farm it.

Mom shared Dad's dreams concerning the farm, as well as dreams of a family that was loving and whole. Her dreams were of happiness as much as of achievement.

Thus when we were growing up we were allowed to dream our dreams and to share them, if we liked. As with most growing children, our dreams changed and grew with us — at various times we aspired to be sea captains, railroad engineers, soldiers or airplane pilots. Sometimes we even dreamed of being farmers.

It was fairly late in my boyhood that I started dreaming of being an artist — or more specifically, a cartoonist. This was only after I had been encouraged by my elders as they saw me spending more and more time with paper and pencil and crayons.

The first of my drawings that attracted any attention was a "mural" on the papered wall of the library of our farm home. I must have been about three years old at the time. I ran out of drawing paper and still having crayon left, was attracted to the great expanse of wall space (as I still am). With the crayon I made a drawing of a man with a head, a nondescript body, and two stick legs with potato-like

93

feet. The right arm ended in a fat hand that resembled the feet except for several stick fingers that bristled from it. Since I hadn't planned well, there still was a lot of unused wall on the left side of my figure. So with the crayon, I started a line in the vicinity of the left shoulder and walked the length of the room making an extremely long arm ending in a hand that appeared to be a distant relative of the other one.

I don't remember being punished for my bit of interior decoration, but I was disappointed by Mom's negative reaction to it. From then on I was provided with plenty of drawing paper in the form of the blank side of sale bills and other used paper. As I got older I drew more and more, not because I wanted to make drawings as such, but because it was a way to visualize the things in my head — imagination put to paper.

This preoccupation with pencil and paper attracted attention and encouragement from my parents, teachers, friends and relatives and it soon became a foregone conclusion that I was to be an artist — if I wasn't already. There were times when the "great expectations" of these benevolent conspirators caused me almost to wish I didn't have this talent they all talked about. I didn't feel comfortable in being one of whom much was expected.

One afternoon I was working at the kitchen table on the rigging of a model ship when a family friend dropped in to see my mother. It bothered me that she was disappointed to find me "wasting my time" on something like that rather than working on the clay busts of Julius Caesar, Abe Lincoln and Franklin Roosevelt that I had temporarily set aside. At that time I could not reassure her with what I've come to know — the small ship I was building was but another facet of the same creative expression as was sculpting the clay busts.

The clay I was attempting to fashion into the likenesses of those famous personages was some Dean and I had dug out of the creek bank in our pasture at a place we called Rusty Cove. It took a lot of processing to clean the roots and little nodules of a rust-like substance from it. We first had done this refining to use the clay in making little bricks to build our "village" along the creek bank.

The clay busts were never fired, but after they had become thoroughly dry, I painted them. Lincoln and Roosevelt were painted with brown enamel, but Julius Caesar was given a coat of gold paint.

In due time Caesar found his way into the office of Superintendent Rankin at the high school. While he was in that auspicious place he seemed to have no positive effect on my struggles with Latin I and II.

Grandma Crow was one of my most enthusiastic early supporters. She was my first patron, buying one of my drawings. I don't remember the drawing nor do I remember how much she paid for it. I'm sure it was not much as she had pitifully little. Through Montgomery Ward mail order house she bought me my first drawing board. I still use it. It is battered and stained and filled with thousands of thumb tack holes, but I'd not part with it for any amount of money.

From my earliest memory, the *Des Moines Daily Register* was the main source of our news (we had no radio then). The trip to the mailbox at the end of the lane every noon was certain to be rewarded with the newspaper. And, periodically, the *Saturday Evening Post, Good Housekeeping, Literary Digest* and *Wallaces Farmer* also appeared. However, it was the *Daily Register* which exerted the most influence on me, especially the editorial cartoon which was featured in the middle of the upper half of the front page. These daily drawings signed "J.N. Ding" were the first thing I not only looked at, but poured over with great attention, studying every line. Often I copied his drawing with a soft, black pencil trying to get the same effect he did with pen and ink. The results were poor, but I kept trying and after some time began to do fairly well at copying. Then I tried doing cartoons of my own. These were indeed sickly efforts.

All of this copying, while not original, was a valuable learning experience and beneficial to me.

Virginia Allinson, Mom's best friend, knew a friend who knew Ding and since she was making a trip to Des Moines, she offered to take some of my drawings to show him. The following weekend Mom invited Allinsons to dinner and Virginia gave a full report of her visit with the great Ding and his reaction to my drawings.

My head was practically spinning as I hung on each word she related from Ding. It was hard to take part later as the other kids tried to interest me in play. This was not because the report was that good on my drawings, but simply due to the fact I had made contact with my idol. What Ding had said was that yes, I did have talent but that I had a lot of hard work ahead of me. He admonished me not to draw so much out of my head but to draw constantly from life. As encouragement he sent along a small pocket sketch pad, a sheaf of newsprint and some soft drawing pencils. I corresponded with Ding several times after that proxy introduction and my drawings and his comments on them went back and forth through the mails during the next few years.

In country school I made cartoons for our little hectographed school paper that was published occasionally. In high school the art program fell victim to the Depression years and was dropped from the curriculum after I'd been enrolled only a few

COME ON, GRANDPA — WHAT ARE Y' THINKIN' ABOUT?

BOB ARTLEY

WORTHINGTON DAILY GLOBE

weeks. But my teacher had me drawing posters for ballgames, plays, etc. I also became staff artist on *The Student Prints*, our mimeographed school paper.

One day in Miss Dunn's English class we were given the assignment to write a short essay in class. It was very difficult for me to write on the spot like that so after a few moments of desperation I drew a cartoon of my predicament and at the end of the class period turned that in.

I didn't know what the teacher's reaction to that bit of whimsey would be and the next day when she came to me in the assembly I was quite apprehensive. To my surprise, she liked the cartoon and suggested I do one daily to be displayed in a frame at the front of the assembly. This seemed quite a challenge, but I agreed to try it. For my last two years in high school my homework was drawing a cartoon for the next day. I did miss now and then, but not often. Most of the topics I dealt with were school-related, but some were of national and world events. In looking back, they were a pretty sorry collection, but I was getting experience and much encouragement to make cartooning my life's work.

After my graduation from high school I no longer had the front of the assembly as a place to display my cartoons. But Kermit Driere, the owner of a popular eating place across the street from the school, asked for a weekly cartoon to display in his establishment. Those were the first cartoons I ever did for pay — not much pay by today's standards, but it was something and made me a professional.

When I was about seventeen I made a pilgrimage to Des Moines to see the great Ding. I had written to him asking for an appointment and haunted our mailbox the next several days until the reply came. No one could have been more exultant than I was as I read and re-read the letter on my way from the mailbox to the house to share it with my family. Ding had written that he'd be glad to see me and suggested a date.

The alarm went off at three a.m. on the appointed day and I sprang from my bed and was soon dressed in the clothes I'd laid out the night before. After seeing that I had a clean handkerchief and insisting that I take a sandwich in case I got hungry, Mom bid me goodby and Dad drove me to Hampton to catch the four a.m. southbound Jefferson Lines bus for Des Moines.

The bus depot was only two or three blocks from the *Register and Tribune* building where Ding had his office. Since the hour was too early for any of the stores or offices to be open, I walked back and forth, up and down Locust street with my packet of drawings under my arm, looking in shop windows.

The morning sunlight was touching the tops of

some of the smog-stained buildings that made a canyon of the street. But down on the street level, where noise and confusion reigned as delivery trucks and trolley cars vied for position with gears grinding, horns blowing and bells clanging, everything was in shadow. The office workers and shop girls were piling out of the street cars and hurrying on their way to work. I tried to stay out of their way and hoped I didn't look too green and countrified to them.

I thought of how back home, a hundred miles north, the same sunlight was dispersing the morning mists across the cornfields and meadows and how its warm beams would be streaking from behind the barn across the farmyard and onto the lawn and against our old white house. The familiar scene in my mind's eye made me feel very much out of place. I wondered if I really wanted to be a cartoonist after all, if it meant living and working in a city.

When the clock in the jewelry store window across the street told me it was eight o'clock I entered the lobby of the *Register and Tribune* building and searched out J.N. "Ding" Darling on the directory. I contemplated the elevators but decided on the stairs and climbed to the eleventh floor. Ding's office was indeed there but not yet open; with my packet of drawings across my lap, I sat on the top step and waited.

Shortly before nine the elevator door opened and a woman emerged, glanced curiously at me and unlocked and entered Ding's office.

After waiting what I judged to be a decent interval I drifted into the office and with my heart in my throat announced who I was. She didn't immediately introduce herself and I guessed that she must be Miss Hauts, since that was the name on her desk. I mumbled something about having a letter in my pocket saying I had an appointment to see Ding that very morning.

Subsequent to that first encounter, I had many occasions to visit with Merle Hauts and found her to be a warm, friendly person. But that morning she seemed very cold and efficient and protective of her boss's interests. She informed me that he would see me for a few minutes but couldn't be kept long as he had this day's cartoon to do. She said I should be seated and wait since he hadn't come in yet.

Time dragged on and the silence seemed awkward to me. I thought it would be nice to start up a conversation. I speculated as to how it looked like a nice day. Miss Hauts gave a curt agreement but obviously was not encouraging any chatter. I recomposed myself and waited in silence.

When Ding finally breezed into the office the atmosphere changed. He was a large, broad-shouldered man with a friendly face and a warm, firm handshake. He put me at ease at once, giving me the feeling that this was but a continuation of our friendship through our correspondence. He led the way into his office and motioned me to a large leather davenport and asked to see my drawings.

Those moments in Ding's office reinforced my dream of being a cartoonist. Here was one of the world's greatest treating me as if I and my drawings were worthy of his time and attention. He went over each drawing, pointing out where it was faulty and commenting favorably whenever he could find something to praise. He turned some of the drawings over and with a few deft strokes of a soft pencil showed how I could have done better.

He asked about my plans for school (advised me not to go to art school as "they'd spoil" me), asked about my family and in general visited as one who had all kinds of time to waste on young, aspiring cartoonists. Suddenly I remembered Miss Haut's stern concern for Ding's tight schedule, so I thanked him for his interview and departed. But before I left I expressed the wish to have a sample of his drawing and, being the generous person he was, he complied by giving me an original cartoon that still hangs in my office.

On the bus trip home that afternoon I went over and over, in my mind, that morning's meeting in Ding's office. I tried to remember and sort out the jumble of words and impressions that poured in upon me in those few moments I was there. I thought of his warning about an art school casting me in their mold; about his advice to "draw, draw, draw from nature"; to take a liberal arts course in college, getting all the history, literature, economics and political science I could.

While I found the world of books and ideas much to my liking, I never had been considered studious and the thought of such an endeavor was not altogether appealing. My primary interest was making pictures, whether they were cartoons or illustrations for books and publications I wasn't sure. I thought of his warning that a great deal of hard and at times discouraging work lay ahead of me. I thought of the price I'd have to pay to leave behind the soil I loved to work and live amid the concrete and asphalt of the city.

How was I to explain all this to my family who would be eagerly awaiting my report at the supper table that evening?

I was glad I couldn't afford to go to college that September but was going to be at home for a year. It would give me a chance to get my dreams straightened out and adjusted to the real world — while working the soil of those beloved acres one more season.